LIVING ON THE RAGGED EDGE

COMING TO TERMS WITH REALITY

BIBLE STUDY GUIDE

From the Bible-teaching ministry of

Charles R. Swindoll

INSIGHT FOR LIVING

These studies are based on the outlines of sermons delivered by Charles R. Swindoll. Chuck is a graduate of Dallas Theological Seminary and has served in pastorates for over twenty-two years, including churches in Texas, New England, and California. Since 1971 he has served as senior pastor of the First Evangelical Free Church of Fullerton, California. Chuck's radio program, "Insight for Living," began in 1979. In addition to his church and radio ministries, Chuck has authored twenty books and numerous booklets on a variety of subjects.

Chuck's outlines are expanded from the sermon transcripts and edited by Bill Watkins, a graduate of California State University at Fresno and Dallas Theological Seminary, with the assistance of Bill Butterworth, a graduate of Florida Bible College, Dallas Theological Seminary, and Florida Atlantic University. Bill Watkins is presently the director of educational resources, and Bill Butterworth is currently the director of counseling ministries at Insight for Living.

Creative Director:	Cynthia Swindoll
Editor:	Bill Watkins
Associate Editor:	Bill Butterworth
Copy Supervisor:	Wendy Jones
Editorial Assistants:	Becky Anderson and Julie Martin
Communications Manager:	Carla Beck
Communications Coordinator:	Alene Cooper
Art Director:	Ed Kesterson
Production Artist:	Becky Englund
Typographer:	Trina Crockett
Cover Designer:	Michael Standlee
Cover:	G. Robert Nease Photography
Production Supervisor:	Deedee Snyder
Printer:	R. R. Donnelley & Sons Co.

An album that contains twenty-four messages on twelve cassettes and corresponds to this study guide may be purchased through Insight for Living, Post Office Box 4444, Fullerton, California 92634. For information, please write for the current Insight for Living catalog, or call (714) 870-9161. Canadian residents may direct their correspondence to Insight for Living Ministries, Post Office Box 2510, Vancouver, British Columbia, Canada V6B 3W7, or call (604) 669-1916.

Unless otherwise identified, all Scripture references are from the New American Standard Bible, © The Lockman Foundation 1960, 1962, 1963, 1968, 1971, 1972, 1973, 1975, 1977. Used by permission.

ISBN 0-8499-8212-X

Table of Contents

Living on the Ragged Edge

To anyone who thinks the Bible is out of touch with our times, I would say "Just read Ecclesiastes!" This Old Testament book is like an ancient journal, covering a segment of Solomon's life which most of us would rather forget. But God has preserved it because of its relevance. You will be amazed to see how much Solomon's thoughts sound like today's overworked, aggressive, success-oriented executive who attempts to find satisfaction in his or her achievements.

Here is under-the-sun, horizontal living. Here is the hedonistic lifestyle in the raw. Here is every attempt to find happiness without God. Here is emptiness personified. Here is life . . . on the ragged edge.

May our Lord use these studies to convince all of us that life is one miserable, futile existence apart from the centrality of Christ and the joy He alone can give. Please do pray that each lesson will reach those who are working overtime to find meaning and purpose . . . pray that they will hear and heed the truth of God's relevant book.

Chuck Swindoll

Putting Truth into Action

Knowledge apart from application falls short of God's desire for His children. Knowledge must result in change and growth. Consequently, we have constructed this Bible study guide with these purposes in mind: (1) to stimulate discovery, (2) to increase understanding, and (3) to encourage application.

At the end of each lesson is a section called **Living Insights.** There you'll be given assistance in further Bible study, thoughtful interaction, and personal appropriation. This is the place where the lesson is fitted with shoe leather for your walk through the varied experiences of life.

In wrapping up some lessons, you'll find a unit called **Digging Deeper.** It will provide you with essential information and list helpful resource materials so that you can probe further into some of the issues raised in those studies.

It's our hope that you'll discover numerous ways to use this tool. Some useful avenues we would suggest are personal meditation, joint discovery, and discussion with your spouse, family, work associates, friends, or neighbors. The study guide is also practical for church classes, and, of course, as a study aid for the "Insight for Living" radio broadcast. The individual studies can usually be completed in thirty minutes. However, some are more open-ended and could be expanded for greater depth. Their use is flexible!

In order to derive the greatest benefit from this process, we suggest that you record your responses to the lessons in a notebook where writing space is plentiful. In view of the kinds of questions asked, your notebook may become a journal filled with your many discoveries and commitments. We anticipate you will find yourself returning to it periodically for review and encouragement.

Bill Watkins
Editor

Bill Butterworth
Associate Editor

LIVING ON THE RAGGED EDGE

COMING TO TERMS WITH REALITY

Journal of a Desperate Journey
Survey of Ecclesiastes

Have you ever wanted to be free from all your responsibilities, to unshackle yourself from those demands that weigh your life down? Have you ever gotten the itch to strike out on your own so that you could fulfill some of those dreams which now only collect dust in the recesses of your mind? Have you ever wondered if your current lifestyle should be traded in for a newer and more exciting one? If you answered yes to any of these questions, you are not alone. Many people are dissatisfied, frustrated, even bored with their lives. Some of these individuals choose to live out their days without making any serious attempt to alter them. Others try numerous ways to interject adventure and excitement into their humdrum existence. But few, if any, go as far to find lasting satisfaction in life as King Solomon did. He went through a maddening period in his adult life when everything lost its luster. During this time, he called some of the most basic assumptions about existence into question. With clenched fists and cynical words, he sneered into the face of God and sought to enjoy life apart from Him. Solomon kept a divinely inspired journal of his desperate journey, known today as Ecclesiastes. As we meditate on its content, we will quickly discover that Solomon's experience is very much a reflection of our own. And we shall see that life cannot be meaningful and purposeful if it is lived apart from God.

I. An Introduction to the Journal

Before we turn our attention to the thoughts recorded in Ecclesiastes, let's glean some essential information about the book's author and central theme.

A. Who wrote it? Nowhere in this journal does the author give his name. However, he does tell us many things about himself that help us arrive at a well-founded conclusion concerning his identity. For example, he calls himself *Qōhelet,* a Hebrew term usually translated "the Preacher" (1:1–2, 12; 7:27; 12:8–10). Because the writer refers to himself in this way, his journal was titled *Ecclesiastes,* which means "one who calls an assembly," by the translators of the Septuagint—an ancient Greek version

1

of the Hebrew Old Testament.[1] The author also identifies himself as a "son of David" (1:1), a "king in Jerusalem" (v. 1), and a "king over Israel in Jerusalem" (v. 12). He adds that he was the wisest person who had ever ruled Jerusalem (v. 16); a builder of great projects (2:4–6); an owner of many slaves, sheep, and cattle (v. 7); a man of much wealth (v. 8); and a possessor of a large harem (v. 8). He sums up his self-description in this way: "I became great and increased more than all who preceded me in Jerusalem. My wisdom also stood by me" (v. 9). No one who reigned in Jerusalem during the Old Testament era fits this portrait better than Solomon. Indeed, so impressive was this man and his kingdom that foreign dignitaries of his day stood in awe of him and sought his counsel (cf. 1 Kings 10). His empire became a synonym for unparalleled greatness.[2] Solomon had the intellectual prowess, the financial resources, and the political power to pursue whatever he desired. And that he did. The Book of Ecclesiastes is a record of his pursuits and the lessons he learned.

B. What is its main theme? The primary message of Ecclesiastes is given in chapter 1, verse 2:

"Vanity of vanities," says the Preacher, "Vanity of vanities! All is vanity."

The Hebrew term rendered *vanity* is used elsewhere in Scripture to denote a breath, a wind, or a vapor (see Prov. 21:6, Isa. 57:13). In Ecclesiastes, Solomon usually uses the word in a metaphorical sense to mean "purposeless, meaningless" (cf. Eccles. 1:14; 2:11, 26; 4:4, 16). He tells us that nothing a person does "under the sun" has any real worth—that it's all empty (1:2–3). In other words, the total value of man's endeavors performed apart from God is zero!

---

1. More information on the Septuagint and other early versions of the Scriptures can be found in these sources: *A General Introduction to the Bible,* by Norman L. Geisler and William E. Nix (Chicago: Moody Press, 1968), chaps. 16–30; *A Survey of Old Testament Introduction,* by Gleason L. Archer, Jr., rev. ed. (Chicago: Moody Press, 1974), chap. 3; *History of the New Testament in Plain Language,* by Clayton Harrop (Waco: Word Books, 1984).

2. Two other sections of Scripture that give an account of Solomon's reign are 1 Kings 1:1–11:43 and 2 Chronicles 1:1–9:31. In recent history, archaeological discoveries have confirmed the biblical record of Solomon's wealth, power, and prestige. Some books that clearly present this data and convey its significance are these: *Treasures from Bible Times,* by Alan Millard (Belleville: Lion Publishing, 1985), pp. 105–11; *Rocks, Relics and Biblical Reliability,* by Clifford A. Wilson, Christian Free University Curriculum (Grand Rapids: Zondervan Publishing House; Richardson: Probe Ministries International, 1977), chap. 8; "Solomon," by Edwin Yamauchi, in *The New International Dictionary of Biblical Archaeology,* edited by Edward M. Blaiklock and R. K. Harrison (Grand Rapids: Regency Reference Library, Zondervan Publishing House, 1983), pp. 419–22.

C. Why does it picture life as pointless? Solomon gives many reasons to support his verdict on life "under the sun," but one is predominant throughout his journal: *From a purely human perspective, life is just a repetitive cycle of events; it neither possesses nor gives lasting value or satisfaction* (see 1:2–11). Therefore, whatever man does is futile. Solomon states it this way: "I set my mind to seek and explore by wisdom concerning all that has been done under heaven.... I have seen all the works which have been done under the sun, and behold, all is vanity and striving after wind" (vv. 13–14).

II. The Flow of the Journal

Although Solomon was a believing sinner, what he wrote in Ecclesiastes was superintended by the holy, all-knowing God. The result was a diary that presents the truth about human life as it is lived apart from God. Let's take a general survey of this journal so we can gain a basic understanding of its progression of thought. The chart on Ecclesiastes found at the end of this lesson is a graphic presentation of what is explained below.

A. Introducing the journey (1:1–11). In these opening verses of Solomon's journal, we read that all human tasks done "under the sun" are in vain (vv. 2–3). The general support for this assessment is the wearisome cycle of life as displayed in both the world around us and our constant inability to find lasting satisfaction in our toil (vv. 4–11). *It's the Pits Never Enough Do enough Empty*

B. Pursuing and exploring (1:12–6:9). In this section Solomon recounts his attempts to find ultimate value and enduring happiness apart from a consistent walk with God. He discovered that the pursuit of wisdom and knowledge ends in "much grief" and "increasing pain" (1:12–18). He found that the paths of pleasure and possessions are futile and unprofitable (2:1–11). The certainty of death for both the wise man and the fool drove Solomon to the conclusion that a wise lifestyle is just as purposeless as a foolish one (vv. 12–17). Labor and its fruits were also explored and found to be grievous and empty (2:18–3:22). The injustice of oppression and the accumulation of wealth were seen to bring largely frustration and dissatisfaction (4:1–16, 5:10–6:9).

C. Reflecting and summarizing (6:10–11:6). By the time we reach this section of the journal, we find Solomon drawing a series of conclusions and lessons from his attempt to live "under the sun." The central thrust of his assessment is this: *Lasting purpose and fulfillment can be found only in a trusting relationship with God.* Nothing less will do.

D. Being young and growing old (11:7–12:8). Toward the end of his musings, Solomon admonishes the young to remember their Creator before age and death overtake them.

E. Drawing some final conclusions (12:9–14). At the close of his journal, the wise Preacher gives two bottom-line exhortations to all: "Fear God and keep His commandments" (v. 13).

III. The Journal's Relationship to Our Journey through Life

Perhaps few of us have viewed life with the stark realism of a "Solomon." But if we are honest with ourselves, we will not deny the accuracy of this book's portrait of life. Solomon's words may be uncomfortable, even difficult to hear, but they present the raw truth about life's emptiness when it is lived apart from God. Thinking back on what we have learned so far, we can draw at least three conclusions from Solomon's experience and apply them to our own.

A. The sensual lure of something better tomorrow robs us of the joys offered today. The temptation to seek greener pastures may be unavoidable, but we can refuse to become its prey. And once we choose to live for today, rather than for tomorrow, we will find it easier to be content.

B. The personal temptation to escape is always stronger than the realization of its consequences. Seldom do we look beyond anticipated, immediate satisfactions to detrimental, ultimate consequences. However, if we alter our thinking in this regard, we will take a firm step toward seeking the eternal values in life.

C. The final destination, if God is absent from the scene, will not satisfy. Emptiness and a fleeting sense of contentment pervade a life acted out apart from God's perspective and approval. The only cure for futility and dissatisfaction in our lives is a consistent walk of faith with the living God.

Living Insights

Study One

With this first lesson we embark on a journey to find meaning and value in all aspects of life. Indeed, the central question Ecclesiastes addresses may be put this way: Is life worth living?

• Let's conduct a brief survey of the book. Copy the following chart into your notebook. Read Ecclesiastes 1–6, paying careful attention to what they have to say about the bad—life without God—and the good—life with God. Then jot down in the appropriate column the news you have read. This will aid you in getting better acquainted with the book.

Living on the Ragged Edge—Ecclesiastes			
Bad News	Verses	Good News	Verses

Living Insights

How are you doing in your search for good news and bad news? Let's continue our survey.

• Make a copy of this chart in your notebook, or simply expand the chart you constructed in study one. Now, dig into Ecclesiastes 7–12. Keeping the same pattern, look for both the bad and the good news, and fill in the appropriate columns with your findings.

Living on the Ragged Edge—Ecclesiastes			
Bad News	Verses	Good News	Verses

LIFE ON THE RAGGED EDGE

Survey of Ecclesiastes

WRITER: Solomon
DATE: About 925 B.C.
MESSAGE: Apart from God, man is miserable and life is meaningless
KEY VERSE: 2:11
KEY WORDS: *vanity, labor, do not know*

Possible Reasons for Preserving the Book:

- To present a formal treatise on the vanity of life without God
- To convey a sustained dialogue between a teacher and his pupil
- To provide a bold autobiography of Solomon's life
- To paint a literary portrait of any life lived apart from God
- To communicate a divine warning to all who are tempted to seek satisfaction without a reliance on God

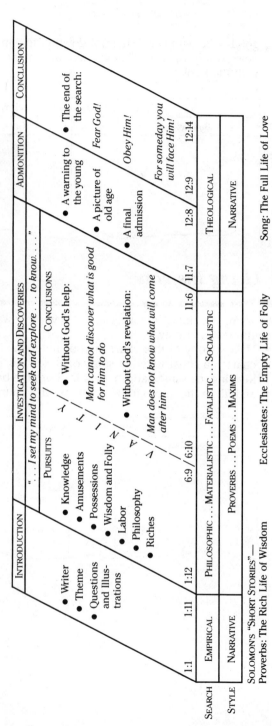

INTRODUCTION — 1:1 / 1:11 / 1:12

- Writer
- Theme
- Questions and Illustrations

INVESTIGATION AND DISCOVERIES

"*. . . I set my mind to seek and explore . . . to know. . . .*"

PURSUITS:
- Knowledge
- Amusements
- Possessions
- Wisdom and Folly
- Labor
- Philosophy
- Riches

CONCLUSIONS:
- Without God's help: *Man cannot discover what is good for him to do*
- Without God's revelation: *Man does not know what will come after him*

VANITY

6:9 / 6:10 / 11:6 / 11:7

ADMONITION — 12:8 / 12:9

- A warning to the young
- A picture of old age
- A final admission

CONCLUSION — 12:14

- The end of the search: *Fear God! Obey Him! For someday you will face Him!*

	SEARCH	STYLE
EMPIRICAL	NARRATIVE
PHILOSOPHIC . . . MATERIALISTIC . . . FATALISTIC . . . SOCIALISTIC	PROVERBS . . . POEMS . . . MAXIMS
THEOLOGICAL	NARRATIVE

SOLOMON'S "SHORT STORIES"—

Proverbs: The Rich Life of Wisdom Ecclesiastes: The Empty Life of Folly Song: The Full Life of Love

Chasing the Wind
Ecclesiastes 1:1–18

The monotonous drag of everyday life is an undeniable fact of reality. To verify it, all you need to do is look around. How many people do you know who awake each morning motivated about the day? How many individuals can you name who genuinely enjoy their occupation or anticipate a new week with delight...who feel challenged and excited about their marriage...or who consistently insert creative ideas and activities into their days to keep life full of zest and enthusiasm? Aside from a few exceptions, most people merely exist with a quiet yet pervasive sense of desperation. They see no future in their employment, little hope for their marriages, a lack of challenge in their pursuits, and a strong feeling of doubt that their lives will ever change for the better. For many people, life is nothing more than futility and boredom. Not even the enjoyment brought by leisurely vacations, extravagant possessions, sexual escapades, delicious food, and professional entertainment bring lasting satisfaction. Is this the assessment of a disgruntled pessimist? Not at all! It's the conclusion of an ancient sage named Solomon who saw the true vanity of human existence as it is lived out "under the sun." The opening section of his journal, Ecclesiastes, exposes the realities of life and tells the truth about existence apart from God. Let's take the time to understand his message and apply his insights.

I. Exposing Four Lies about Life
There are at least four falsehoods about life that are popularly accepted today as true. One is, "Laugh and the world laughs with you; cry and you cry alone." Actually, the opposite of this is true. People tend to rally when tragedy strikes, but hesitate to glory in the successes of others. Another common lie is, "Every day in every way our world is getting better and better." A person would have to be divorced from reality to believe such a tragic illusion. "There's a light at the end of every tunnel" is still another lie about life. What we usually find is not more light but mistier fog and greater darkness. The last falsehood we will expose is this: "Things never are as bad as they seem, so dream, dream, dream." The first part is often true. Things usually are not like they appear to be. In reality, they are often worse, and dreaming will not make them better. Why do people embrace these lies and encourage others to believe them as well? The reason is simple. They want to believe that there is purpose and happiness in this life if they keep on hoping. But the hope they cling to and exercise ignores the fact that the world is corrupt, work is unfulfilling, and people are selfish. Life on planet Earth is not a bowl full of cherries; it's the pits. Instead of enrichment and joy, we find emptiness and sorrow.

II. Telling the Truth about Existence

Unlike those who perpetuate delusions about life and offer us only a false hope, Solomon gives us the straight facts about human existence, regardless of how disturbing we may find them. And he speaks as a man with experience. His father, David, had fought the battles that secured Israel's safety and left a large estate that made Solomon wealthy. So after Solomon accepted the reins of leadership, he had the luxury of ruling over a nation that was free from war for about forty years. In addition, he had the freedom to take money that was slotted for Israel's defense and rechannel it into his pursuit of happiness apart from God. What he learned as he butted his head against the immovable wall of reality has been inerrantly recorded in Ecclesiastes for all of us to read. Let's plumb the depths of its opening verses so that we can face life as it is.

A. **A basic premise** (vv. 1–3). After identifying himself as "the Preacher, the son of David, king in Jerusalem," the writer goes on to give us his overall assessment of life.

> "Vanity of vanities," says the Preacher,
> "Vanity of vanities! All is vanity."

In Hebrew literature, words are repeated for emphasis. What Solomon is saying here could be put this way: "All is utterly vain . . . completely empty . . . absolutely zero!" Life appears to have substance and the ability to bring contentment. But in reality, it has no value and no power to give true satisfaction. Even our labors done "under the sun" yield no "advantage" (v. 3). The Hebrew word translated *advantage* means "that which is left over when the transaction is complete." When all is said and done, there will be nothing left that will give us a sense of accomplishment and gratification. Life lived on a purely human plane is unfulfilling, purposeless, and worthless.

B. **Examples of futility** (vv. 4–11). What evidence does Solomon present in support of his premise? As we might expect, he directs us toward reality and points out several examples of vanity "under the sun."

1. **The passing of generations** (v. 4). People are born, and people die. So the cycle goes. "But the earth remains forever." And since the Fall of Adam and Eve, even the earth has been "subjected to futility" (Rom. 8:20; cf. Gen. 3:17–18). So neither man, who is impermanent, nor creation, which is permanent, escape the futility of existence.

2. **The cycles of nature** (vv. 5–8a). The ceaseless rhythm of nature also demonstrates that activity in and of itself produces nothing of ultimate value—indeed, it brings only wearisome monotony. For example, the sun rises and sets, only to rise again and repeat the process (Eccles. 1:5). The

"swirling" wind blows to the south, then to the north, but it never arrives at a fixed goal or finds lasting rest (v. 6). Even the rivers accomplish nothing of lasting worth, for they flow into the sea yet never fill it. And once they have arrived at their destination, they continue to roll along, only to evaporate and become rain that falls to the earth, hence beginning the cycle again (v. 7). No wonder Solomon writes, "All things are wearisome; / Man is not able to tell it" (v. 8a).

3. **The curiosity of man** (v. 8b). Another example of vanity is man's quest for knowledge. When his curiosity is aroused, he seeks answers to his questions. But these answers only raise more questions, which place man on a treadmill to know still more. And so the cycle goes, never bringing any true satisfaction or rest.

4. **The absence of something new** (vv. 9–11). Finally, without denying human creativity, Solomon points out that "there is nothing [completely] new under the sun" (v. 9b). "That which has been is that which will be, and that which has been done is that which will be done" (v. 9a). Old Testament scholar Donald R. Glenn explains what Solomon is driving at here.

> For example, man's journey to the moon and the discovery of America, though different, were both explorations of distant places, involving adventure and risk. And the invention of dynamite and of the atomic bomb shared the element of discovering an 'explosive.' Thus what is true in the realm of nature—the constant repetition of previous accomplishments—is in essence true of the activity of people;... all things produce only indescribable weariness and lack of satisfaction.[1]

But people fail to acknowledge the absence of newness because they do not remember former events and accomplishments (vv. 10b–11).

C. **The searcher and his pursuits** (vv. 12–18). At this juncture, Solomon turns our focus from his general observations about nature and man to some specific conclusions about his own pursuits. He informs us that when he was king "over Israel in Jerusalem," he determined "to seek and explore by wisdom concerning all that has been done under heaven" (vv. 12–13a).

1. Donald R. Glenn, "Ecclesiastes," in *The Bible Knowledge Commentary: Old Testament Edition,* edited by John F. Walvoord and Roy B. Zuck (Wheaton: Victor Books, 1985), p. 980.

The Hebrew term for *seek* carries the idea of theoretically investigating the roots of a matter, whereas the word translated *explore* conveys the thought of experientially examining all sides. In short, Solomon set out to research thoroughly every approach to life and then to actively immerse himself in each one. To many people, this would seem an exciting and rewarding adventure. But Solomon discovered that, in reality, it is simply not so. He describes it as "a grievous task which God has given to the sons of men to be afflicted with" (v. 13b). He concludes that "all the works which have been done under the sun" are "vanity and striving after wind" (v. 14). Even the search for wisdom, madness, and folly turned out to be a meaningless endless chase after the wind (v. 17). Why? "Because in much wisdom there is much grief, and increasing knowledge results in increasing pain" (v. 18). What a bleak picture! But the quest for satisfaction can be no other way if we seek happiness without God at the center of our lives.

III. Thinking Through the Practical Ramifications

Solomon has delivered a despairing yet accurate report of life as lived solely from a horizontal perspective. Fortunately, however, two thoughts emerge from his observations that point to something better.

A. If there is nothing but nothing under the sun, our only hope must be above it. Just as we are born with the need to satiate our hunger, so we have an innate need to find purpose and value in life. It stands to reason that if we cannot satisfy our drive for meaning and worth on a purely horizontal plane, then we must be able to fulfill it on the vertical level. Our frustration and despair should turn our eyes from earth to heaven, from man to God, from ourselves to Christ. Only *above* the sun does hope shine eternal.

B. If a man who had everything investigated everything visible and found nothing of value, then the one thing he needed must have been invisible. Like Solomon, we could explore every visible realm of stimulation and still find no satisfaction. But would that mean that there is no lasting joy to be had? Not at all! What it does indicate is that the physical realm was never designed to bring us the happiness we long for. The visible world was created to direct us to the One who desires to abundantly satisfy our thirst for contentment—the invisible God (cf. Matt. 6:25–34, Acts 14:15–17, Rom. 1:19–20, Heb. 11:3, 6). And He promised that if we come to Him by accepting His Son as our Savior, then we will never thirst again (John 4:13–14).

Living Insights

Study One ━━━

Before we finish reading even the first three verses of Ecclesiastes, we can sense futility. As Solomon muses, life can be as frustrating as chasing the wind. Let's dig a little deeper into the first chapter of this book.

- An understanding of the text is often enhanced by asking questions about the verses. The following chart will help you categorize your questions. Copy it into your notebook, then read chapter 1 and jot down the questions that come to your mind. Once you complete this step, return to the text and try to find the answers. Some of your queries may not be answerable without additional information. A good Bible dictionary can usually supply the data you need. Two excellent ones are *Unger's Bible Dictionary,* by Merrill F. Unger (Chicago: Moody Press, 3d ed., 1966), and *The Zondervan Pictorial Bible Dictionary,* edited by Merrill C. Tenney (Grand Rapids: Regency Reference Library, Zondervan Publishing House, 1967).

Ecclesiastes 1:1–18	
Questions	Answers
Who?	
What?	
Where?	
When?	
Why?	
How?	

 Living Insights

Study Two ━━

"And I set my mind to seek and explore by wisdom concerning all that has been done under heaven" (Eccles. 1:13a). Once that noble goal was accomplished, Solomon had to conclude that human wisdom does not bring relief from life's frustrations.

- How does *intellectualism* affect your life? Are you placing a higher value on the quest for knowledge than you should? Or have you mistakenly opted for the opposite extreme, concluding that "ignorance is bliss?" Do you feel you have a healthy, balanced approach toward learning? Take a page of your notebook and write this heading at the top: "My Pursuit of Satisfaction through

Knowledge." Then, write down your feelings on this issue. Perhaps this lesson has taught you something about intellectualism. If so, include it in your notebook.

Digging Deeper

Some years ago, C. S. Lewis penned words that are directly relevant to the conclusion of our lesson. Note carefully what he said:

> "Creatures are not born with desires unless satisfaction for those desires exists. A baby feels hunger: well, there is such a thing as food. A duckling wants to swim: well, there is such a thing as water. Men feel sexual desire: well, there is such a thing as sex. If I find in myself a desire which no experience in this world can satisfy, the most probable explanation is that I was made for another world. If none of my earthly pleasures satisfy it, that does not prove that the universe is a fraud. Probably earthly pleasures were never meant to satisfy it, but only to arouse it, to suggest the real thing."[2]

Interestingly enough, it was the desire to satisfy his longing for joy that eventually drove C. S. Lewis to Jesus Christ. Throughout history, the search for enduring happiness has led countless individuals to rest their faith in the living God. This pervasive human quest has also provided philosophers, theologians, and apologists alike with a reasonable argument for the existence of the Christian God. If you would like to dig deeper into the details of this support for God's existence as well as into the accounts of some individuals who became believers through such evidence, then we would recommend that you begin with the books named below. Non-Christians will discover in these sources more reasons to believe in Christ. Christians will find these materials strengthening to their faith and encouraging to their witness to others.

- **Sources on the Search for Satisfaction and the Existence of God**
  Augustine, Saint. *Confessions.* Translated by R. S. Pine-Coffin. The Penguin Classics. New York: Penguin Books, 1961.
  Evans, C. Stephen. *Existentialism: The Philosophy of Despair and the Quest for Hope.* With a response by William Lane Craig. Rev. ed. Christian Free University Curriculum. Grand Rapids: Zondervan Publishing House; Dallas: Probe Ministries International, 1984.

---

2. C. S. Lewis, *Mere Christianity* (New York: Macmillan Publishing Co., Inc., 1952), p. 120.

Geisler, Norman L. *Is Man the Measure? An Evaluation of Contemporary Humanism.* Grand Rapids: Baker Book House, 1983. Chap. 13.

Geisler, Norman L. *Philosophy of Religion.* Grand Rapids: Zondervan Publishing House, 1974. Chaps. 1–4.

Geisler, Norman L., and Feinberg, Paul D. *Introduction to Philosophy: A Christian Perspective.* Grand Rapids: Baker Book House, 1980. Chap. 22.

Kreeft, Peter J. *Heaven: The Heart's Deepest Longing.* San Francisco: Harper and Row, 1980.

Lewis, C. S. *The Four Loves.* New York: Harcourt Brace Jovanovich, 1960.

Lewis, C. S. *Mere Christianity.* New York: Macmillan Publishing Co., Inc., 1952. Pp. 74–78, 118–21.

Lewis, C. S. *Surprised by Joy: The Shape of My Early Life.* New York: Harcourt Brace Jovanovich, 1966.

Purtill, Richard L. *C. S. Lewis's Case for the Christian Faith.* San Francisco: Harper and Row, 1981. Chap. 2.

Purtill, Richard L. *Reason to Believe.* Grand Rapids: William B. Eerdmans Publishing Co., 1974. Chap. 9. Although this book is currently out of print, it can be found in stores carrying used books.

Trueblood, D. Elton. *Philosophy of Religion.* Reprint. Grand Rapids: Baker Book House, 1973.

Eat, Drink, . . . and Be *What?*

Ecclesiastes 2:1–11

The maxim of today's generation can be stated in these six words: If it feels good, do it! Sometimes we hear them spoken openly and defiantly. Other times, they are subtly implied in the print we read or the programs we watch. But whether this principle is whispered or shouted, the message it conveys is being actively lived out and promoted in our day. However, we would be naive to think that the contemporary emphasis on pleasure is new or peculiar to our fast-paced society. Hedonism has been around for centuries; it was even adopted by Solomon about three thousand years ago. He decided to seek satisfaction through the pursuit of pleasure. With intense commitment and tremendous financial resources, he set out to experience self-gratification to the utmost. And what did he discover? Could pleasure satisfy his deepest needs? Could purpose and contentment be found in a playboy lifestyle? Let's join Solomon for a walk down the hallway of his reflections. There we will learn the answers to these questions and their relevance to our lives.

I. A Quick Review

As the king of Israel, Solomon had the greatest political clout in the nation and ready access to whatever he desired. He also reigned during a period of peace, which heightened his opportunity to enjoy life to its fullest. Solomon took advantage of this time, but he failed to use it wisely. Rather than deepen his relationship to God, he sought to find happiness apart from Him. In the first chapter of his journal, we saw how Solomon tried to accomplish this through educational advancement and experiential exploration. But the end of his search was that "all is vanity and striving after wind" (Eccles. 1:14). The pursuit of contentment "under the sun" is purposeless and valueless.

II. An Open Invitation

After stating his general conclusion about life without God, Solomon goes on to describe the specific trails he explored that led him to declare the futility of existence. The first path he mentions is pleasure. Solomon tells us that he came to a point where he said to himself, " 'Come now, I will test you with pleasure. So enjoy yourself' " (Eccles. 2:1a). He not only fantasized about tantalizing his senses but immersed himself in ecstatic delights, making his wildest dreams become reality. And what did he find? Emptiness. To put it in his words, "It too was futility" (v. 1b). At this point, we might think: Wait, perhaps Solomon didn't cover all the bases; could he have missed a sensual experience that would have altered his conclusion? But

Solomon seems to have anticipated this response, for he takes ten verses just to detail his escapades regarding pleasure. Let's consider what he says.

A. **Wild 'n crazy fun 'n games** (vv. 2–3). One avenue Solomon tried was laughter. Perhaps he called in a steady stream of court jesters, clowns, and assorted comedians. Maybe he even attempted to look at only the funny side of life. Whatever the specifics were, his assessment of this way to happiness was blunt and decisive: "I said of laughter, 'It is madness,' and of pleasure, 'What does it accomplish?' " By saying this, Solomon does not deprecate a healthy sense of humor, but he points out that a life geared only to fun and games will not bring lasting satisfaction. Well, if lighthearted amusement was not the answer, perhaps it could be found in a bottle. Solomon tried this as well: "I explored with my mind how to stimulate my body with wine while my mind was guiding me wisely, and how to take hold of folly, until I could see what good there is for the sons of men to do under heaven the few years of their lives." We should not come away from this passage thinking that Solomon became a lush. Old Testament exegete H. C. Leupold states in this regard that these words refer "to a consumption of wine which enables a man to get the highest possible enjoyment by a careful use of it, so that appetite is sharpened, enjoyment enhanced, and the finest bouquets sampled and enjoyed. Approximating or falling into drunkenness is plainly not under consideration."[1] So did becoming a connoisseur of fine wine yield the joy Solomon sought? Again, the answer is no (v. 11).

B. **Houses, plants, parks, and pools** (vv. 4–6). Next, Solomon embarked on a construction enterprise that rivaled anything else that had been done in Israel (cf. 1 Kings 4–10, 2 Chron. 2–9). Here in Ecclesiastes 2, he summarizes his activities this way: "I enlarged my works: I built houses for myself, I planted vineyards for myself; I made gardens and parks for myself, and I planted in them all kinds of fruit trees; I made ponds of water for myself from which to irrigate a forest of growing trees" (vv. 4–6). But did any of these projects give him a sense of accomplishment and worth? No, not a one (v. 11).

C. **Slaves, animals, singers, and wives** (vv. 7–8). So Solomon filled his meaningless life with purchases of "male and female slaves, . . . and flocks and herds larger than all" who had preceded him in Jerusalem. He also collected "silver and gold, and the treasure of kings and provinces." He even surrounded himself with "male and female singers and the pleasures of

H. C. Leupold, *Exposition of Ecclesiastes* (Grand Rapids: Baker Book House, 1952), p. 60.

men—many concubines." In another context we read that "he had seven hundred wives, princesses, and three hundred concubines" (1 Kings 11:3a). Probably no one who has ever lived has had such an abundance of erotic experiences at his bidding. And yet, they left him empty, bored, and frustrated. In fact, the many women he loved eventually "turned his heart away" from God (v. 3b).

D. The "good life" (vv. 9–10). Continuing on in Ecclesiastes 2 Solomon says "I became great and increased more than all who preceded me in Jerusalem. My wisdom also stood by me." To this he adds, "All that my eyes desired I did not refuse them. I did not withhold my heart from any pleasure, for my heart was pleased because of all my labor and this was my reward for all my labor." In the eyes of many, Solomon had achieved the good life. He experienced it for all it was worth. And what did he gain? Good feelings. We cannot deny that sensual pleasures are gratifying. However, the thrill they produce is fleeting, while the guilt and anguish illicit pleasures usually bring lingers on.

III. It's Time to Face the Truth

Solomon's verdict on the pleasure-seeking lifestyle deserves to be heard by the widest possible audience: "Thus I considered all my activities which my hands had done and the labor which I had exerted, and behold all was vanity and striving after wind and there was no profit under the sun" (Eccles. 2:11). His words speak the truth. And we would be wise to hear and heed them. Let's wrap up Solomon's discoveries in three statements that will help us face life as it really is.

A. Sensual pleasures make promises that lack staying power. It doesn't matter if the alluring thrill is alcohol, drugs, sex, or anything else. Such pleasures never deliver the satisfaction they promise.

B. Sensual pleasures offer to open our eyes, but in reality they blind us. Propagators of hedonism tell us that if we will follow our urges and lusts, a whole new world of incredible pleasure will unfold. But what actually happens is that a lifestyle of self-gratification leads us away from the truly important things in life—from family, friends, and God.

C. Sensual pleasures disillusion us, making us cover up artists. The pursuit of epicurean dreams may satisfy for a time, but eventually it will leave us empty. That's a hard fact to face, and many people refuse to do so. Rather than admit that their escapades have been futile, they con themselves and others with a hypocritical cover-up, pretending to have found true satisfaction. Good feelings that don't last, blindness to what's important, and acting out a lie—are these worthwhile results for living a hedonistic lifestyle? Certainly not . . . but they are all a person will ever have to show for chasing the wind.

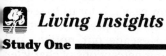

Living Insights

Study One ▬▬▬▬▬▬▬▬▬▬▬▬▬▬▬▬▬▬▬▬▬▬▬▬▬▬▬▬▬▬

As our study has revealed, Solomon certainly had the pick of fun, games, projects, pools, slaves, songs, and the overall good life! Let's go back to the historical section of the Old Testament to see how his story developed.

- First Kings 1–11 gives us a concise summary of Solomon's life. As you read these chapters, use a copy of the following chart to record significant facts about this king and his reign. This exercise will help establish some important groundwork that will be valuable throughout our entire study.

The Life of Solomon—1 Kings 1–11	
Important Notes on Solomon's Life	Scripture References

Living Insights

Study Two ▬▬▬▬▬▬▬▬▬▬▬▬▬▬▬▬▬▬▬▬▬▬▬▬▬▬▬▬▬

In the last lesson we paused to consider our attitude toward *intellectualism* in light of the first chapter of Solomon's journal. In Ecclesiastes 2, we have dealt with the pursuit of *pleasure*. With the help of the following questions, think through your perspective on this issue.

- Is pleasure important to you? Why or why not?
- How do you find pleasure? List specifics.
- How do you overemphasize pleasure in your life?
- How is pleasure underemphasized in your life?
- What helps you achieve balance in this area?
- Is there a close association between your pursuit of pleasure and your involvement in the world's system?
- What is the most significant lesson you learned from this study on pleasure?

More Miles of Bad Road
Ecclesiastes 2:12–26

"God sees not as man sees, for man looks at the outward appearance, but the Lord looks at the heart" (1 Sam. 16:7b). How easy it is for us to see the obvious while overlooking the significant. People's appearances get our attention, but their deeper qualities often escape our notice. And unfortunately, instead of choosing to sharpen our perceptions of character, we tend to take advantage of man's shallow perspective. We frequently act out a role, seeking to falsely impress others rather than truly reveal ourselves. In doing this, we may appear to be stable and successful when we are actually troubled and frustrated. Some of us peel off our masks and admit our struggles from time to time, but few of us remove them permanently and make vulnerability a hallmark of our lives. Solomon chose to take this step when he made his journal available for all to read. The result is a book that reveals the hopelessness of finding genuine happiness apart from God. As we continue our journey through Solomon's diary, we will discover several more miles of bad road. But we will see that his search is not one lacking flashes of positive insight. Toward the end of chapter 2, he begins to hint at what satisfies when life lived "under the sun" does not.

I. A Glance Back
Without hesitation, Solomon has admitted his inability to find satisfaction in intellectual pursuits, comic relief, building projects, and sensual pleasures. Although some of these pursuits produced good feelings for a time, all of them were but "vanity and striving after wind" (Eccles. 2:10–11).

II. The Search Continues
Running into a few dead ends was not going to stop Solomon. There were other roads to travel, and he set out to explore them. Ecclesiastes 2:12–23 recounts three of the routes Solomon took and what he discovered along the way.

A. Wisdom compared to foolishness (vv. 12–17). In these words the Preacher recalls the first decision that confronted him:

> I turned to consider wisdom, madness and folly, for what will the man do who will come after the king except what has already been done? And I saw that wisdom excels folly as light excels darkness. The wise man's eyes are in his head, but the fool walks in darkness. (vv. 12–14a)

Solomon thought about whether to adopt a lifestyle marked by wisdom or one characterized by foolishness. Since he was the king, no one in his nation could dictate his destiny; the choice rested with him alone. At first he reasoned that wisdom is better than folly, for a wise person has the foresight to avoid danger, while a fool does not. The former thinks clearly and sees insightfully, but the latter thinks cloudily and sees obscurely. However, in the final analysis, "one fate befalls them both"— death (v. 14b). In spite of the education we pursue, the responsibility we shoulder, or the common sense we exercise, our end will be the grave just as will the fool's. When this truth dawned in Solomon's mind, he said to himself, " 'Why then have I been extremely wise? ... This too is vanity' " (v. 15). Indeed, "there is no lasting remembrance of the wise man as with the fool, inasmuch as in the coming days all will be forgotten" (v. 16a). Not only will the wise and foolish die, but they will be forgotten. Therefore, the person who lives responsibly has no advantage over the individual who lives irresponsibly. This realization drove Solomon to hate life and declare once again that "everything is futility and striving after wind" (v. 17).

B. The immediate compared to the ultimate (vv. 18–21). Since satisfaction was not found in wise living, perhaps it could be gained through the joy of leaving one's wealth to one's children, friends, or successors. Solomon considered this option as well and concluded that it too was futile. Notice what he said:

> Thus I hated all the fruit of my labor for which I had labored under the sun, for I must leave it to the man who will come after me. And who knows whether he will be a wise man or a fool? Yet he will have control over all the fruit of my labor for which I have labored by acting wisely under the sun. This too is vanity. Therefore I completely despaired of all the fruit of my labor for which I had labored under the sun. When there is a man who has labored with wisdom, knowledge and skill, then he gives his legacy to one who has not labored with them. This too is vanity and a great evil.

Burning the midnight oil, developing great plans, risking hard-earned funds, skipping much-needed vacations, worrying about competitors ... then, when we least expect it—death. The wages we have reaped are passed on to others, and we have no assurance that they will be used wisely. So what's the value in our labors? From a purely human perspective, there is none.

C. Daily work compared to evening relief (vv. 22–23). Perhaps Solomon has drawn his conclusions too hastily. Certainly he has reasoned well so far, but there is another alternative that he should have considered. Couldn't his successors have been trained to handle his fortunes responsibly? Wouldn't that have given him peace and satisfaction after a hard day's work? We might think so, but Solomon concluded otherwise: "For what does a man get in all his labor and in his striving with which he labors under the sun? Because all his days his task is painful and grievous; even at night his mind does not rest. This too is vanity." Solomon may have been thinking about his son, Rehoboam, when he penned these words. After Rehoboam was given the right to rule by Solomon, he chose to heed foolish counsel that plunged Israel into civil war within the first year of his rule. This internal strife made Israel more vulnerable to foreign aggression, especially from Egypt. In order to avoid an invasion, Rehoboam plundered the temple Solomon had built and used the gold he took to pay off the Egyptian army (1 Kings 12:1–24, 14:21–31). What a tragedy! But we cannot guarantee that what happened to Solomon's estate will not occur to the fruits of our labors after we pass on.

III. Some Flashes of Insight

It seems there is no way we can obtain meaning, value, . . . purpose in our lives. For in Ecclesiastes so far, every path we have explored has led only to emptiness and despair. Is there no hope? Can we ever find enjoyment in life? Surprisingly enough, in the midst of this bleak series of frustrating scenes, Solomon receives three flashes of insight that reveal the way to lasting satisfaction.

A. **There is nothing inherent in humanity that makes it possible for us to extract enjoyment and purpose from the things we do.** Translated literally from the original Hebrew text, Solomon's words read this way: "There is nothing in a man to eat and drink and tell himself that his labor is good" (Eccles. 2:24a). Human beings do not have the natural capacity to draw out genuine joy from their endeavors, so the human energy exerted to accomplish this goal is wasted. However, all is not lost. Let's push on and observe Solomon's next flash of insight.

B. **Enjoyment is God's personal gift.** The enablement for man to find satisfaction in life comes "from the hand of God. For who can eat and who can have enjoyment without Him?" (vv. 24b–25). If the Lord is not at the center of a person's life, contentment will be fleeting, at best. However, when Christ is sitting on the throne of one's life, an abiding joy will pervade it regardless of the external circumstances (cf. Phil. 4:11–13). But this is not all a consistent walk with God can bring. Solomon unveils one more insight in Ecclesiastes 2.

C. **Those who are right with God derive the benefit of everyone's labor.** Solomon writes, "For to a person who is good in His sight He has given wisdom and knowledge and joy while to the sinner He has given the task of gathering and collecting so that he may give to one who is good in God's sight. This too [namely, the sinner's amassing of wealth] is vanity and striving after wind" (v. 26). Those who do not order their lives according to God's standard will never enjoy the benefits of their toil. Yet, those who have Jesus Christ as the nucleus of their lives will ultimately profit from the work of others. Of course, this does not mean that Christians never travel bad roads or run into dead-end streets. But believers do have the ability to persevere through tough times and even reap benefits from them. Unbelievers, on the other hand, face only endless miles of futility with no way of escape except through Christ. On what road are you?

Living Insights

Study One

So far in our journey we've seen futility in knowledge, pleasure, and possessions. The latter verses of chapter 2 speak of the futility in *labor*. This theme will be developed even further as we proceed in the book.

- Copy the following chart into your notebook. As you read through Ecclesiastes 2:12–26, jot down words from the text that are important to a proper understanding of the passage. Then, seek to discover each word's meaning from the verses themselves. If that's difficult, consult a Bible dictionary. Finally, write down a statement telling why each word is significant.

Ecclesiastes 2:12–26			
Verses	Key Words	Definitions	Significance

Continued on next page

🐟 Living Insights

This lesson concludes with some flashes of insight. We haven't seen much of this until now, so it's worth our time to dig deeper. Think through the following:

• Pick one of the three applications at the close of the outline that best represents an area of your life which needs work. How can you bring to light this issue in your life? What are some specific, concrete items you can begin working on over the next few days? Take a pencil and paper and sort out some of your thoughts through writing. Make this lesson personal.

Do You Know What Time It Is?

Ecclesiastes 3:1–11

Regardless of our birthplace, occupation, age, or religious persuasion, we all have at least one thing in common—time. All of us have twenty-four hours each day to spend as we please, but we cannot credit any of today's hours to tomorrow's account. No matter how hard we may wish for it to be so, we know there will never be more than twenty-four hours in a day. Furthermore, we get only one opportunity to use each minute we have; once it has passed, it is gone forever. The writer of Ecclesiastes realized the importance of time and the central role it plays in human life. He recorded some of his thoughts about the relationship between time and man's activities in the first several verses of chapter 3. In drawing his observations to a close, he set forth two conclusions that could alter our outlook on life and our relationship to God. So let's zero in on this portion of God's Word and remain open to what the Lord desires to say through it.

I. Time: A Few Pertinent Questions

Before we resume our study of Ecclesiastes, we need to get a firm grip on a rather slippery subject—time. We can do this by addressing the three questions given below.

A. What is time? One clear expression of the nature of time is this: "a measurable period during which events occur." As we can see from this definition, time involves process or change. If all things that change ceased to exist, so would time. One cannot exist without the other.[1]

B. Why is time so important? Among the many reasons we could cite, one stands out: Time is significant because it is completely irretrievable. Once a unit of time has been used, it cannot be recaptured or relived.

C. When will time end? The instruments man has invented to measure time will one day lose their usefulness. For one day the most dependable timepiece that has ever been created—the movement of the planets—will stop. And when that occurs, time as we know it will come to an end.

---

1. It is interesting to note that many Christian theologians have concluded from the nature of time and the immutability of God that time and the universe were created simultaneously. In other words, there was no time before God brought the universe into existence. An implication of this line of reasoning is that God is timeless, not temporal (cf. Gen. 1:1, Heb. 1:10–12, Jude 25). Some excellent discussions on this issue can be found in these sources: *City of God,* by Saint Augustine, 11.6; *Summa Theologica,* by Saint Thomas Aquinas, 1.46.3; *Biblical Words for Time,* by James Barr, rev. ed., Studies in Biblical Theology (Naperville: Alec R. Allenson, Inc., 1969); and *The Doctrine of God,* by Herman Bavinck, translated by William Hendriksen (Grand Rapids: Baker Book House, 1977), pp. 145–52.

II. Life: Measured according to Its Events

After Solomon ponders the idea of being unable to enjoy life apart from God (Eccles. 2:24–25), he breaks life down into measurable segments that he calls "events." Here is how he opens chapter 3: "There is an appointed time for everything. And there is a time for every event under heaven" (v. 1).

A. All-pervading opposites (vv. 2–8). In these verses Solomon sets forth fourteen pairs of opposite events, each of which are to occur at appointed times. The fact that he mentions them in a multiple of seven and begins his list with birth and death is highly significant. "The number seven suggests the idea of completeness and the use of polar opposites—a well-known poetical device called merism—suggests totality (cf. Ps. 139:2–3)."[2] So even though every conceivable event of life is not named in these verses from Ecclesiastes 3, the whole of life is definitely in view. Let's take a closer look at the opposites Solomon mentions.

1. **"A time to give birth, and a time to die"** (v. 2a). Certainly, we have no control over our birth. Neither can we lengthen our days beyond the time God has chosen for them to end (8:8; cf. Job 14:5). Both events are subject to God's control.

2. **"A time to plant, and a time to uproot what is planted"** (v. 2b). These words from Ecclesiastes 3 point out our need to cooperate with the seasons of nature. If we chose to plant or harvest certain crops in the dead of winter, we would lose them. However, we could reap a bumper crop if we prepared the soil, planted the seed, cared for the crop, and harvested its produce at the proper times. Likewise, we dare not ignore the seasons of our lives and fail to cultivate our growth according to God's timetable.

3. **"A time to kill, and a time to heal"** (v. 3a). Life seems to be a strange mixture of battlefields and first-aid stations, murder and medicine. In the same city we can find people who assault others for pay, and those who seek to cure others out of genuine concern. And yet, there are some occasions when it is right to take a human life (see Gen. 9:6, Exod. 21:12–17) and many other times when it is appropriate to restore someone to health (see Matt. 11:2–6, James 5:14–16).

4. **"A time to tear down, and a time to build up"** (v. 3b). Urban renewal is a perfect illustration of what this passage

---

2. Donald R. Glenn, "Ecclesiastes," *The Bible Knowledge Commentary: Old Testament Edition,* edited by John F. Walvoord and Roy B. Zuck (Wheaton: Victor Books, 1985), p. 983.

from Ecclesiastes 3 is talking about. Demolition crews are called in to destroy a structure, then construction crews are sent in to build anew.

5. **"A time to weep, and a time to laugh"** (v. 4a). Events involving death and destruction often cause pain and sadness, while times of birth and restoration usually bring enjoyment and celebration. Occasions that lead to either tears or laughter can be used by God to get our attention, but times of suffering are generally the most effective. C. S. Lewis makes this point well:

> We can rest contentedly in our sins and in our stupidities; and anyone who has watched gluttons shovelling down the most exquisite foods as if they did not know what they were eating, will admit that we can ignore even pleasure. But pain insists upon being attended to. God whispers to us in our pleasures, speaks in our conscience, but shouts in our pains: it is His megaphone to rouse a deaf world.[3]

6. **"A time to mourn, and a time to dance"** (v. 4b). Like the other pairs of opposites we have observed so far, sorrow and joy have appropriate times of expression as well. For example, the loss of loved ones brings grief (cf. John 11:1–44), while the marriage of lovers merits a celebration (cf. John 2:1–11).

7. **"A time to throw stones, and a time to gather stones"** (v. 5a). These words from Ecclesiastes 3 may refer to the gathering of good building materials and the rejecting of faulty construction products. More likely, however, this pair of opposites shares the same meaning as the next set Solomon mentions.

8. **"A time to embrace, and a time to shun embracing"** (v. 5b). The time to embrace can be likened to the time to gather stones, and the time to shun embracing can be linked with the time to throw stones. In other words, there are occasions when we should affirm others and thank them for encouraging us. There are other circumstances, however, when caring confrontation and constructive criticism are needed.

9. **"A time to search, and a time to give up as lost"** (v. 6a). Rescue teams continually face this reality. They need to decide when a search for someone who is lost should continue and when it should cease.

---

3. C. S. Lewis, *The Problem of Pain* (New York: Macmillan Publishing Co., Inc.), p. 93.

10. **"A time to keep, and a time to throw away"** (v. 6b). This can be illustrated with an example from our homes. Most of our garages and closets contain things that have value and should be kept. However, there are also those items that have outlived their usefulness and ought to be cast out.
11. **"A time to tear apart, and a time to sew together"** (v. 7a). This pair of opposites may refer to the preceding set—keeping and throwing out. It also might be associated with the tearing of clothes that accompanied mourning (cf. Job 2:12–13) and the mending of clothes that occurred once the period of mourning ended.
12. **"A time to be silent, and a time to speak"** (v. 7b). In this verse from Ecclesiastes 3, Solomon reminds us that there are times when we should declare our convictions and stand up for what is right. However, there are other occasions when it is wise, considerate, and even loving to remain quiet (cf. Job 2:11–13).
13. **"A time to love, and a time to hate"** (v. 8a). Continuing on in chapter 3 of Ecclesiastes, Solomon observes that expressions of love should mark our lives. On the other hand, he reminds us that we should not fail to express hatred when the circumstance warrants it. For example, acts of injustice, oppression, and prejudice should be hated and withstood.
14. **"A time for war, and a time for peace"** (v. 8b). When tyranny threatens the people of a nation, war may become a necessary measure of self-defense. However, when there is an opportunity for differences to be resolved and rights restored, peace should be sought so that war can be averted.

B. All-encompassing questions (v. 9). Two questions seem to leap from this section of Solomon's journal. One of them is stated and the other only implied. The first is this: *What is the profit?* When life is examined and reduced to its essentials, what gain or value is there in a person's endeavors? The answer is *none.* Solomon indicates this in his list of opposites. Each pair contains a negative and a positive that seem to cancel out each other. The net result, therefore, is zero. Human life has its endless cycles just as nature does (cf. 1:3–11). As such, man's existence is empty and profitless. The second question is this: *What is the purpose?* Where is life going? As the pairs of opposites suggest, human life is going nowhere. We experience birth and death, and have no control over either. So what makes us think that there is any value to be found in between these events? All we discover are ceaseless cycles of love and hate,

26

planting and reaping, building and destroying, laughing and weeping.

C. **All-important conclusions** (vv. 10-11). How can we find profit and purpose under the sun? We can do it only by looking beyond the sun and into heaven. We must transcend our human perspective and adopt a divine viewpoint. Solomon points this out as he draws this portion of his journal to a close. Here is what he says: "I have seen the task which God has given the sons of men with which to occupy themselves. He has made everything appropriate in its time. He has also set eternity in their heart, yet so that man will not find out the work which God has done from the beginning even to the end." Let's briefly note the three conclusions Solomon makes.

1. **God has made everything appropriate in its time.** The Hebrew word translated *appropriate* may also be rendered *beautiful.* Our lives may sometimes look like a confused collage of clashing colors; but if we were to step back and consider them from God's vantage point, we would view them as an ordered mosaic of complementary hues. Only the divine perspective can reveal the meaning and worth of our lives. On its own, the human perspective will see only vanity.

2. **God has put eternity in our hearts.** The Lord has created us with an insatiable curiosity about our future and an intense longing for heaven. We may seek to satisfy our curiosity through faulty means—such as horoscopes and palm-reading—or we may strive to fulfill our longing for heaven with something bound only to earth. But we will not discover the right answers to our questions about tomorrow or satisfy our desire to spend forever with God unless we search for Him in His way. As the writer of Hebrews states, "Without faith it is impossible to please Him, for he who comes to God must believe that He is, and that He is a rewarder of those who seek Him" (Heb. 11:6). If we want to ready ourselves for eternity, then we must accept God's Son, Jesus Christ, by faith (John 1:12–13, 3:16).

3. **We cannot discover God's eternal plan.** Only the Lord knows His plan from beginning to end. But He has mercifully revealed the crucial aspects of His overall plan to us in His Word. As a result, we can find purpose and worth in life if we will seek to understand and apply the Scriptures. However, if we choose to remain ignorant of the truth they unveil and confirm, then we will see only futility in our lives.

Living Insights

"There is an appointed time for everything. And there is a time for every event under heaven" (Eccles. 3:1). With that introduction, Solomon delivers one of the better-known poetic sections of Scripture.

- Make a copy of the following chart. Ecclesiastes 3:2–8 consists of fourteen couplets—twenty-eight statements of activity. Jot down the phrases in the left-hand column of your chart, then conduct a scriptural search for other verses that back up the ideas presented by Solomon.

Ecclesiastes 3:2–8	
A Time to ...	Biblical Examples

 Living Insights

Were you able to find biblical examples for the twenty-eight statements? Let's try a different approach that will make Solomon's observations more personal.

- Once again, copy this chart into your notebook. This time, however, look for examples from *your life* to illustrate the statements in Ecclesiastes. Some may be incidents you've *experienced;* others may be things you've *observed.* Try to fill in something for each statement.

Ecclesiastes 3:2–8	
A Time to ...	Personal Examples

Interlude of Rare Insight
Ecclesiastes 3:11–15

Three of the largest money-making movies of all time began with the words, "A long time ago in a galaxy far, far away." The creative genius behind these films, George Lucas, has transported millions of moviegoers from the dull, routine lifestyle they live on earth to a fantasy world filled with excitement and suspense. For many people, this has become a common method of escape. However, once the adventure ends, the viewers find themselves again stuck on earth, still surrounded by the problems that plague them. Such is reality on the horizontal plane. It can only be transcended temporarily . . . or so it seems. In the middle of Ecclesiastes 3, Solomon changes his perspective from the horizontal to the vertical, from a purely human one to a divine one. The result is an insightful interlude that begins to show us how we can consistently enjoy life under the sun.

I. Life without God

Before we consider the hope Solomon reveals, let's briefly review the despair he has exposed. The Preacher has described life without God in a number of ways. He has said that "all is vanity" (1:2b) and that "there is nothing new under the sun" (v. 9b). He has demonstrated that "all the works which have been done under the sun [are] . . . vanity and striving after wind" (v. 14). Solomon has also noted that wisdom brings "grief, and increasing knowledge results in increasing pain" (v. 18). He has recounted that pleasure-seeking is futile and profitless (2:1–2). He has even shown that both a wise lifestyle and a foolish one are vain and that human labor is painful, grievous, wearisome, and pointless (2:18–23). In short, this Old Testament sage has told the truth about life lived apart from God— namely, that it is the pits. And God has designed it to be that way. He has created us with a God-shaped vacuum that only He can fill. And until He does, life is little more than a hell on earth.

II. Life with God

In Ecclesiastes 3:11–15, Solomon unexpectedly changes the pace. He directs our thoughts from considering life without God to examining life with God. This radical change in focus points the way toward meaning, hope, encouragement, and best of all, deliverance from a life full of despair. Solomon weaves his comments through three subjects—what God makes, what God gives, and what God does. Let's investigate each one.

A. What God makes (v. 11). When we lift our eyes from earth and begin to see life with a heavenly perspective, we discover that *God makes "everything appropriate [or beautiful] in its time"* (v. 11a). A New Testament passage that amplifies this theme is Romans 8:28, which reads, "And we know that God causes all things to work together for good to those who love God, to those who are called according to His purpose." These words from the Apostle Paul do not suggest that everything is good any more than Solomon's words imply that everything is appropriate. The Scriptures definitely acknowledge that evil and ugliness exist, and they also warn us not to call evil good, or good evil (Prov. 17:15, Isa. 5:20). On the other hand, they are equally clear in affirming that God will make even the wicked deeds of humans and demons work out for good in His eternal plan. When considered from God's vantage point, the pain we feel and the anguish we suffer—regardless of how purposeless and profitless they may seem—actually make sense and produce value. Solomon also points out that *God makes everybody curious about the future* (Eccles. 3:11b). Because God has set eternity in our hearts, we have an innate desire to see beyond today. But we can despair for tomorrow when we lack the hope to go on. And only the Lord can supply this hope we so desperately need. In fact, He has made us in such a way that our thirst to know the future cannot begin to be quenched until we place our trust in Him.

B. What God gives (vv. 12–13). As Solomon continues to look at human life from the divine perspective, he observes that the Lord gives us four gifts. First, *God gives us the ability to rejoice and enjoy life* (v. 12a). But He does not provide it for everyone. Only believers receive this gift, for only they have the perspective and hope needed to sustain a life of joy regardless of their circumstances. Second, *God gives us the ability to do good in our lifetime* (v. 12b). Solomon is not talking about our capability to treat someone kindly so that we can be treated well in return. That is a selfish "talent" which we have acquired as a consequence of sin. Rather, Solomon is referring to our God-given potential to do good for others whether or not they reciprocate. Furthermore, this ability is to be utilized in our lifetime. We cannot do anything to benefit other people when we are "six feet under." *Now* is the time to do good. Third, *God gives us an appetite to eat and to drink* (v. 13a). Practically everyone has the ability to eat, but far fewer people are able to really enjoy and appreciate their food. The latter capability is a gift of God, while the former is not. Fourth, *God gives us the ability to see good in all our labor* (v. 13b). Again, the under-the-sun perspective of man is this: I earn what I get. But the above-the-sun perspective that God grants us can be put in these words: You are given what you will never deserve and can never earn—gifts such as forgiveness, everlasting life, and hope.

C. What God does (vv. 14–15). In these verses Solomon delineates four truths about God's actions. The first two highlight the quality of God's activities, while the last two emphasize the activities themselves. Let's note each one. Solomon first mentions that God's works are *permanent* (v. 14a). They will endure when everything else passes away. Next Solomon informs us that God's deeds are *thorough and complete* (v. 14b). They never lack anything, nor are they ever superfluous. Furthermore, *God performs things that cultivate our respect for Him* (v. 14c). For example, His creation is so incredible that even many non-Christians stand in awe of its splendor and its Creator. And finally, *God patiently repeats things until they are learned* (v. 15). We often try to pass by what He is desiring to teach us. But the Lord graciously keeps bringing us back to these lessons until we learn them permanently.

III. Life from God

Let's wrap up our study of these verses with two specific thoughts.

A. Life from God comes from outside this galaxy—not from within it. Positive thinking, higher education, good books, self-help, or any other means under the sun cannot bring us everlasting life. The abundant, satisfying life is found above the sun in God through His Son, Jesus Christ. As the Lord says, "'I am the way, and the truth, and the life; no one comes to the Father, but through Me'" (John 14:6; cf. 10:28).

B. Life from God is supernatural power now, not a vague force limited to a long time ago. The greatest evidence of power is change. And God has been in the business of changing lives since the dawn of human history. But He does not dispense His life-changing power to those who do not want it. Certainly, He seeks to persuade all people to repent of their sins and to accept His forgiveness (Matt. 9:35–38, 23:37, 28:18–20; John 15:8–11). However, He never compels individuals; He asks them to trust freely in His Son for their salvation (John 1:12–13; Acts 17:2–4, 10–12; Rom. 10:9–15). If you have not placed your faith in Christ as your Savior, will you do so today?

Living Insights

Study One ▬▬▬▬▬▬▬▬▬▬▬▬▬▬▬▬▬▬▬▬▬▬▬▬▬▬▬▬

These verses in Ecclesiastes 3 are like a breath of fresh air. In contrast to the usual perspective of life under the sun, we see some valuable words on what God makes, what God gives, and what God does.

- There's real depth in Ecclesiastes 3:11–15. Frankly, a casual reading would leave us with only a surface understanding of the text. This study provides an excellent occasion to consult other Bible translations and paraphrases. Look up the passage and read it unhurriedly and thoughtfully. Often reading another version brings a set of verses to life! Set this as your goal: to better understand these five verses.

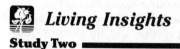 *Living Insights*

Study Two

Life and power from God are available now through faith in His Son. It's certainly more exciting and possible than a vague force from a galaxy far, far away! Read over the list of advantages to life with God. Place a (√) by the ones you would like to be more aware of in your life. Spend some time in prayer talking to God about these particular aspects. Think about some specific ways you can begin implementing His power in your life.

- God makes everything beautiful in its time.
- God makes everybody curious about the future.
- God gives the ability to rejoice.
- God gives the capacity to do good.
- God gives the ability to appreciate food and drink.
- God gives perspective for seeing good in our labor.
- God performs works that are permanent.
- God performs works that are thorough and complete.
- God performs acts that cultivate our respect for Him.
- God patiently repeats lessons until they are learned.

Confessions of a Cynic

Ecclesiastes 3:16–22

We all like stories, especially those that have tidy endings. It usually doesn't matter to us if the characters fall prey to harrassment and hardship during the tale as long as right wins over wrong in the end. A story doesn't even have to conclude happily for us to enjoy it. But it dare not end unjustly. If only reality were like that—how wonderful it would be. Unfortunately, all of us realize that in life the helpless are frequently pushed around, the cruel often escape justice, and many who appear to be generous are actually greedy and oppressive. Living with injustice long enough can cause a person to become disillusioned and cynical. This can occur quite easily in an individual who lacks a divine perspective. King Solomon stands out as a perfect example of this. When looking at life from an under-the-sun perspective, he sees only barrenness. There is no lasting satisfaction to be found. In fact, what he discovers are the terrible effects of injustice, affliction, and suffering. The world is out of control; wrong reigns and right is trampled underfoot. This state of affairs makes Solomon cynical. Rather than falling to his knees in dependence on God, he stands defiantly, shaking his fist at heaven. Is there a better way to face inequity, oppression, and atrocity? There is, and Solomon the cynic shows it to us. But first, he helps us understand the underlying cause of pessimism and considers some solutions that can dissolve it.

I. The Problem That Creates Cynicism

The matter that sent Solomon into a slump of cynicism is stated in various places throughout his journal. We might summarize what he says like this: Although people long for wrongs to be righted, their desire is often crushed between the oppressive rocks of wickedness. Here are some passages from Ecclesiastes that illustrate this point through Solomon's eyes.

> I have seen under the sun that in the place of justice there is wickedness, and in the place of righteousness there is wickedness. (3:16)
> Then I looked again at all the acts of oppression which were being done under the sun. And behold I saw the tears of the oppressed and that they had no one to comfort them; and on the side of their oppressors was power, but they had no one to comfort them. So I congratulated the dead... more than the living.... But better off than both of them is the one who has never existed, who has never seen the evil activity that is done under the sun. (4:1–3)
> If you see oppression of the poor and denial of justice and [of] righteousness in the province, do not be shocked

at the sight, for one official watches over [or, protects]
another official, and there are higher officials over them.
(5:8)
All this I have seen and applied my mind to every deed
that has been done under the sun wherein a man has
exercised authority over another man to his hurt. (8:9)
Whether we think it is fair or not, we must confront the fact that in
our world, evil frequently triumphs over good, injustice routinely
replaces justice, and inequality habitually sweeps aside equality.

II. Does Cynicism Have a Solution?

How can we cope with injustice and not become pessimistic in the
process? Is there a divinely sanctioned solution to our struggle? Yes,
there is, and the Lord graciously reveals it in the words of Solomon.
Let's explore the counsel he renders in Ecclesiastes 3:17–21. What
we will find is that the cure for cynicism is twofold.

A. **Remember that injustice will have only a temporary
reign.** Looking above the sun, Solomon observes that " 'God
will judge both the righteous man and the wicked man,' for a
time for every matter and for every deed is there" (v. 17). We
can restate his meaning with these words: There is a time for
every matter and every deed, be it good or evil. However, wrong
will not go unpunished, and right will not go unrewarded,
forever. Someday the Lord of all will judge the deeds of all and
make everything come out fairly. This perspective should give
us hope and peace.

B. **Realize that injustice reveals man's beastlike
behavior.** Turning his eyes toward earth, Solomon allows his
cynicism to pour forth. In doing so, he unveils a divine purpose
for permitting human injustice. Notice what he writes: "I said to
myself concerning the sons of men, 'God has surely tested them
in order for them to see that they are but beasts' " (v. 18). The
evil we inflict on one another demonstrates the beastly
characteristics of our nature and conduct. Sin eats away at our
humanity so that the more we yield to it the more subhuman
and brutelike we become (cf. Pss. 49:12–20, 73:21–22; Titus 1:12;
2 Pet. 2:12–13; Rev. 13:1–20:10). Now Solomon does not stop by
comparing human life to animal life. He goes on to liken the
destiny of man to the destiny of beasts: "The fate of the sons of
men and the fate of beasts is the same. As one dies so dies the
other; indeed, they all have the same breath and there is no
advantage for man over beast, for all is vanity. All go to the same
place. All came from the dust and all return to the dust"
(Eccles. 3:19–20). But do both man and animal remain in the
grave? Solomon leaves that question open when he writes,

"Who knows that the breath [soul] of man ascends upward and the breath [soul] of the beast descends downward to the earth?" (v. 21). We know from other biblical texts that God extends human life beyond the grave (see 1 Cor. 15:50–57, 1 Thess. 4:13–17, Rev. 20:11–21:8). But these verses in Ecclesiastes point out that, from empirical observation alone, death places man and beast on equal footing. As far as we can observe by watching people and animals die, we have no advantage over beasts; our destiny and theirs is the same—death, nothing more.

III. Hope beyond Cynicism: Some Concluding Thoughts

Solomon closes this section of his journal with some final thoughts on how to deal with injustice and mistreatment. Consider what he says: "I have seen that nothing is better than that man should be happy in his activities, for that is his lot. For who will bring him to see what will occur after him?" (Eccles. 3:22). Notice that Solomon does *not* exhort us to try to understand our circumstances, to retaliate with bitterness, or to retreat into our closets and suffer in resentful silence. What he *does* suggest is that we reject self-pity and revenge, then seek out ways to find the advantages in our disadvantages. In short, we may not be able to alter our lot in life, but we can change our response to it. Let's ask ourselves three questions that can help reorient our hopeless cynicism to hopeful realism.

A. **What is your unjust disadvantage?** Don't answer with a list of petty irritations, but think in terms of major handicaps in your life that you feel have been inflicted upon you unfairly.

B. **When do you plan to replace passive self-pity with active courage?** If you have not already begun to turn from a destructive, woe-is-me attitude to a constructive, enjoy-life-now posture, then start today. The Lord will give you the power to make the change, but you must avail yourself of it through prayer and action.

C. **Have you ever considered the impact your distinctive message could have on the world around you?** The Lord can use your disadvantage—be it physical, emotional, mental, financial, or anything else—to positively impact the lives of others. The only thing that stands in the way is your attitude. Will you change it today?

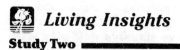

Living Insights

Study One ▬▬

Injustice—the very meaning of the word shouts out, "It's not fair!" We all have our share of disadvantages; thus, it's helpful to get a biblical perspective on the issue.

- Peter's first letter is an epistle on injustice. The Roman emperor Nero was ready to inflict torture on the Christians *simply because they were Christians!* The following chart points us to a couple of passages worthy of further study on this subject. As you read them, look for principles on handling injustice.

Handling Injustice—1 Peter 3:13–17, 4:12–19	
Principles	Verses

Living Insights

Study Two ▬▬▬▬▬▬▬▬▬▬▬▬▬▬▬▬▬▬▬▬▬▬▬▬▬▬▬▬▬▬▬▬▬▬▬▬▬▬▬

As you studied this passage, did you find it uncomfortably relevant to situations in your life? Let's devote our "Living Insights" to serious reflection on the concluding three questions. Copy them into your notebook, allowing plenty of space for your written responses.

- What is your unjust disadvantage?
- When do you plan to replace passive self-pity with active courage?
- Have you ever considered the impact your distinctive message could have on the world around you?

The Lonely Whine of the Top Dog

Ecclesiastes 4:1–8; Luke 12:15–21

We have been inundated with books, seminars, courses, and speeches on the subject of top-level management and success-oriented leadership. The hype has never been greater nor the lure more effective. Indeed, we have largely been convinced that the achievement of an impressive position brings lasting satisfaction and a liberating sense of pleasure. But for the executive, the proverbial pot of gold at the end of the rainbow is not what it appears to be. More often than not, managers have head-on collisions with intense pressure, political rivalry, economic anxiety, and inescapable loneliness. Centuries ago, King Solomon addressed the emptiness of those who make it to the top of their profession. His words live on today. They can make a difference in our lives if we will hear them well and heed their cry.

I. What Ought to Be Isn't What Is

Take several moments to read and ponder these verses from Solomon's journal:

> Then I looked again at all the acts of oppression which were being done under the sun. And behold I saw the tears of the oppressed and that they had no one to comfort them; and on the side of their oppressors was power, but they had no one to comfort them. So I congratulated the dead who are already dead more than the living who are still living. But better off than both of them is the one who has never existed, who has never seen the evil activity that is done under the sun. And I have seen that every labor and every skill which is done is the result of rivalry between a man and his neighbor. This too is vanity and striving after wind. The fool folds his hands and consumes his own flesh. One hand full of rest is better than two fists full of labor and striving after wind. Then I looked again at vanity under the sun. There was a certain man without a dependent, having neither a son nor a brother, yet there was no end to all his labor. Indeed, his eyes were not satisfied with riches and he never asked, "And for whom am I laboring and depriving myself of pleasure?" This too is vanity and it is a grievous task. (Eccles. 4:1–8)

What Solomon says here should be required reading at the finest business schools in the country. His statements ought to be printed in every professional journal subscribed to by the most successful individuals of our day. All college graduates should have these verses inscribed on their diplomas. The problem is that none of these "ought to bes" are a reality, and they probably never will be. Instead, every entrepreneur and every climber of the corporate ladder is enticed by counsel that promises a dream but delivers a nightmare.

II. A Realistic Appraisal

As Solomon looks around, he sees people who have reached the top and those below who are still clawing their way up. He observes military officers, political leaders, and the other "top dogs" of his day and then records what he finds. His appraisal of their lifestyle is not pleasant to read, but it is nonetheless accurate. As we consider it, let's recall that Solomon is speaking as a participant, not merely an observer. He pens these words in Ecclesiastes 4:1–8 while reigning in Jerusalem, experiencing a world of lavish affluence.

A. Oppressive conditions (vv. 1–3). The first scene Solomon recounts is depressing: "I looked again at all the acts of oppression which were being done under the sun. And behold I saw the tears of the oppressed and that they had no one to comfort them; and on the side of their oppressors was power, but they had no one to comfort them." As he views the few in authority making life miserable for the many under them, Solomon is driven to frustration and despair. Notice his reaction: "So I congratulated the dead who are already dead more than the living who are still living. But better off than both of them is the one who has never existed, who has never seen the evil activity that is done under the sun." What a bleak response! And Solomon is not yet finished.

B. Competitive determination (vv. 4–6). Looking out over his world, Solomon encounters another all-too-familiar situation: "And I have seen that every labor and every skill which is done is the result of rivalry between a man and his neighbor. This too is vanity and striving after wind." Solomon is not referring to healthy, ethical competition between large corporations and small businesses. What he has in mind is a one-on-one rivalry of pushing, fighting, and clawing—the vicious determination of two people to outdo one another at any cost. According to the Israelite ruler, this kind of aggressive competition is empty. In fact, those who engage in it are fools. That is what he means when he writes, "The fool folds his hands and consumes his own flesh." Destructive rivalries will not lead to a fulfilled life. People must seek balance in their lifestyle before they can obtain contentment. As Solomon states it, "One hand full of rest is better than two fists full of labor and striving after wind." This truth made such an impression on King Solomon that he speaks of it again in the Book of Proverbs. Consider some of the counsel he gives:

Better is a little with the fear of the Lord,
Than great treasure and turmoil with it. (Prov. 15:16)
Better is a dish of vegetables where love is,
Than a fattened ox and hatred with it. (v. 17)
Better is a little with righteousness,
Than great income with injustice. (16:8)

Burning the candle at both ends and running roughshod over people in an incessant push for success is the formula for exhaustion, loneliness, and a guilty conscience. What a price to pay! Solomon calls this maddening pursuit "vanity and striving after wind" (Eccles. 4:4b).

C. **Personal disillusionment** (vv. 7–8). The top dog Solomon makes one more observation before offering a familiar assessment. In these verses he moves away from considering groups and pairs of individuals, and fixes his gaze on one person. Notice what Solomon says: "Then I looked again at vanity under the sun. There was a certain man without a dependent, having neither a son nor a brother, yet there was no end to all his labor. Indeed, his eyes were not satisfied with riches and he never asked, 'And for whom am I laboring and depriving myself of pleasure?' " Here is the perfect picture of someone who had become a slave to the pursuit of success. Even though he had no family responsibilities, he continued to work long hours and amass more wealth. Yet, he never took the time to ask himself the obvious: "Why am I laboring so hard? Why doesn't my wealth bring the satisfaction I long for? Why am I not slowing down and enjoying myself along the way? Who is going to benefit from my work since I am not?" Rather than evaluate his imbalanced lifestyle, he drove himself into the ground only to become disillusioned and unfulfilled. No wonder Solomon concludes, "This too is vanity and it is a grievous task."

III. A Penetrating Analysis

Before moving on, we need to sit back and think about Solomon's appraisal. He has pegged our society well, hasn't he? Let's face it, most of us are taught that if we work hard enough . . . compete fiercely enough, then we will make it to the top of our profession and there find relaxation and contentment. But what makes us think that if we are not satisfied where we are, we will be satisfied somewhere else? When we look up the ladder of success and examine the lives of those at the top, do we really find many happy, carefree people? No, . . . and if we listen long enough, we will hear their whines of loneliness, disillusionment, and despair.

IV. An Ancient yet Relevant Story

Jesus Christ told a parable that aptly illustrates the tragedy of seeking satisfaction in success. While addressing a large crowd, Jesus was approached by a man who said, " 'Teacher, tell my brother to divide the family inheritance with me' " (Luke 12:13). After posing a question to the man (v. 14), Jesus responded with a warning: " 'Beware, and be on your guard against every form of greed; for not even when one has an abundance does his life consist of possessions' " (v. 15). His words pierced the thin veneer covering the man's request and penetrated to his real motive. Then Jesus proceeded to illustrate His point with this story:

> "The land of a certain rich man was very productive. And he began reasoning to himself, saying, 'What shall I do, since I have no place to store my crops?' And he said, 'This is what I will do: I will tear down my barns and build larger ones, and there I will store all my grain and my goods. And I will say to my soul, "Soul, you have many goods laid up for many years to come; take your ease, eat, drink and be merry." ' But God said to him, 'You fool! This very night your soul is required of you; and now who will own what you have prepared?' So is the man who lays up treasure for himself, and is not rich toward God." (vv. 16b–21)

Material gain will never satisfy our spiritual thirst. Neither will power, prestige, or success. If we pursue these things without God at the center of our lives, we might gain the world for a time, but we could forfeit our souls for eternity (Matt. 16:26).

V. Two Haunting Questions

When we reduce what we have covered to its essentials, two questions emerge that demand soul-searching answers.

A. Are you telling yourself the truth about possessions? Solomon and Christ agree. Material prosperity will never satisfy; only a saving relationship with the Lord will.

B. Are you hearing God's warning about priorities? The Lord must be given first place. Then, and only then, will true satisfaction flood your life (Matt. 6:24–33).

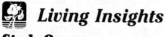 *Living Insights*

Study One ▬▬▬▬▬▬▬▬▬▬▬▬▬▬▬▬▬▬▬▬▬▬▬▬▬▬

"And I have seen that every labor and every skill which is done is the result of rivalry between a man and his neighbor. This too is vanity and striving after wind" (Eccles. 4:4). The phrase "result of rivalry" is intriguing. It speaks of competition, a subject worth analyzing.

- What does the Bible say about competition? Is rivalry good, bad, or both? These questions are more difficult than they may appear. You'll soon discover that Scripture says precious little on the subject! You may want to change your approach and write down what you believe about competition. Then see if you can find Scriptures to generally support your ideas. This is an assignment for a real thinking person. Go for it!

 Living Insights

y

Study Two ▬▬▬▬▬▬▬▬▬▬▬▬▬▬▬▬▬▬▬▬▬▬▬▬▬▬▬▬▬▬▬▬▬

There's a good chance you've experienced the lure of our success-oriented society. It's also quite possible that you have seen the lethal consequences that result. In view of your experiences, write down some of your thoughts on the following suggested topics:

My Attitude toward Possessions

My Attitude toward Priorities

My Attitude toward Success

y
41

One Plus One Equals Survival
Ecclesiastes 4:9–12

The word *lonely* describes one of the most desolate conditions known to man. For many people, loneliness is a way of life, especially for the majority of those who make it to the highest level of their professions. As Solomon finishes describing the grim scene of numerous top dogs, he offers a plan for combatting loneliness that everyone can appropriate. If we take his counsel to heart, we will discover one of the most down-to-earth truths in Scripture—*two really are better than one.* And by applying Solomon's advice along with some other biblical principles, we will begin to experience the cure for loneliness—namely, *companionship.*

I. Some Common Cries of the Lonely

If we were to stop and listen to the lonely people around us, we would probably hear at least three common cries. The first one flows from a heart of *blame.* It says, in effect, "Why don't people love me and help me out of my problems?" But in order to have companionship in times of need, one must cultivate friendships before a crisis. Difficulties do not automatically bring friends. The second common cry could be worded this way: "If only others realized how difficult things are!" This is the lament of *self-pity.* Few responses will ruin a relationship more quickly than this one. In fact, it is an attention-getter that swiftly wears out another person's patience. The third whine comes from a *martyr* complex: "Nobody really cares! I am all alone in this!" Of course, if no one knows about another's heartache, then they certainly cannot be blamed for not responding in a helpful manner. When we need an outstretched hand, we must let it be known.

II. Some Survival Counsel for the Lonely

Bemoaning the fact that we are lonely will not help us. What we must do is recognize that companionship is the solution to our feelings of alienation. We really cannot enjoy life to its fullest as loners. People were created to need other people; we cannot fill that need with ourselves, things, or even God (Gen. 2:7–9, 18–23). In Ecclesiastes 4:9–12, Solomon reiterates this truth and reveals three reasons that friends are a necessity in our lives.

A. A statement of fact. Solomon conveys a truth about reality in these words: "Two are better than one because they have a good return for their labor" (v. 9). The Preacher is not addressing just marriages here, but he is including all kinds of morally responsible companionships. Solomon is telling us that it is better to share our life with another person rather than "go it alone." Existence under the sun can be wearisome, frustrating, grievous, and sometimes treacherous. Having a friend at our side can enable us to survive even our most troublesome days.

B. Reasons two are better than one. Why can a faithful companion make our trek through life easier and more enjoyable? Solomon answers this in verses 10–12. Let's consider what he says.

1. **One provides encouragement when the other is weak.** Whenever we struggle or fail, we need a companion who will not walk away but will stay and lift us up (v. 10a). We may pretend to be rugged survivors and tough-minded winners, but the truth is that we all have weaknesses which call for the strength others can give. And if we don't have anyone to lean on, then what? Solomon tells us: "Woe to the one who falls when there is not another to lift him up" (v. 10b). For the Hebrew term translated *woe*, we could substitute the words *horrors, peril,* or *danger.* We are dependent creatures, and when we choose not to rely on another person, we risk staying down and defeated after we have fallen. But a friend can lift us up, dust us off, and help us get going again.

2. **One gives support when the other is vulnerable.** "If two lie down together they keep warm," says Solomon, "but how can one be warm alone?" (v. 11). This verse refers to more than the provision of body heat for one who is cold. It also includes comforting and supporting a person who is in an unguarded state—one who is confronting a situation that involves potentially threatening elements which will not go away. In our modern world, some examples of such occasions are the first day at a new job, the beginning week in a new school, or an embarrassing encounter in the unemployment line. During times like these we need a friend by our side.

3. **One supplies protection when the other is attacked.** Solomon conveys this reason in verse 12a. These words refer to the fact that the ability of two people to ward off a physical assault is much greater than that of one individual. However, the Preacher's statement is not limited strictly to physical dangers. For instance, a companion can help thwart vicious rumors and other verbal abuses that are launched against us. A Christian friend can also support our spiritual stand against sin and satanic forces (see Eph. 6:10–18, where the Greek pronoun for *you* is plural, thus referring to Christians as a community, not as individuals; cf. Gal. 6:1–2, James 5:19–20).

C. A final comment. If two are better than one, what could be better? Three, of course. As Solomon says, "A cord of three strands is not quickly torn apart" (Eccles. 4:12b). His point is that we should seek to cultivate more than one friendship. Indeed, the more committed companions we have, the less likely we are to suffer the devastating pangs of loneliness.

III. Some Biblical Examples and Practical Principles

Although it's not difficult to hear the truth in Solomon's words, we may need help to apply it. In order to do this, let's look at some men and women in the pages of Scripture who lived out this counsel. From each biblical example, we will be able to draw a relevant principle for our lives.

A. Elijah and Elisha. Some years after the death of Solomon, a prophet named Elijah arose on the scene. During his period of ministry in Israel, he went into the throne room of Ahab and Jezebel and predicted that a severe drought was about to plague the land (1 Kings 17:1). Then the Lord told the prophet to seek refuge by the "brook Cherith, which is east of the Jordan" (v. 3). Elijah did as the Lord commanded, but soon "the brook dried up" as a consequence of the drought (vv. 5–7). Approximately three-and-one-half years later, Elijah confronted the prophets of the false god Baal. He met them on Mount Carmel where he disgraced their god and ended their lives by the power of the one true God (18:16–40). Such an incredible event must have left Elijah physically weak, emotionally drained, and spiritually worn. While he was in this condition, the wicked Queen Jezebel threatened to have him executed within a twenty-four hour period (19:2). Frightened, Elijah fled for his life to Beersheba, left his servant there, and then "went a day's journey into the wilderness" (vv. 3–4a). There he sat down under a tree and asked God to take his life (v. 4b). But the Lord did not grant his request or rebuke him for running from Jezebel. Instead, God granted Elijah enough food and rest to sustain him for a forty-day journey to Mount Horeb (vv. 5–8). Once he arrived at this mountain, he was encouraged by the Lord and then sent away again. It was during his departure that God gave him a friend named Elisha (v. 19). After they met, the text says that Elisha "followed Elijah and ministered to him" (v. 21b). From that moment on, they traveled and served together.

> **Principle One**
> Companions calm the troubled waters of our souls.

B. Naomi and Ruth. Tucked between the books of Judges and 1 Samuel is the brief but powerful Book of Ruth. Its content revolves around two women, Naomi and Ruth. After the death of her husband and two children, Naomi told her two daughters-in-law to return to their homes and begin their lives anew (Ruth 1:3–5, 8–13). One of them did as Naomi had requested, but the other, Ruth, insisted on staying. Ruth spoke to Naomi with words of comfort and assurance: " 'Do not urge me to leave you or turn back from following you; for where you go, I will go, and where you lodge, I will lodge. Your people shall be my people, and your God, my God. Where you die, I will die, and there I will be buried. Thus may the Lord do to me, and worse, if anything but death parts you and me' " (vv. 16–17). Now that's the commitment and support of a true friend!

Principle Two

Companions build bridges of hope and reassurance when we are vulnerable, exposed, and self-conscious.

C. David and Jonathan. A monarch named Saul reigned several years prior to the birth of Solomon. One day King Saul led Israel's army out to engage in battle with the Philistine army (1 Sam. 17:1–3). The Philistines challenged the Jews to send out one from their midst to face Goliath—a huge man and a valiant warrior (vv. 4–10). The Philistines' proposal caused Saul and his army to quake with fear (v. 11). No one in Israel's camp was willing to accept the challenge—that is, not until a teenager by the name of David arrived on the scene. Armed with only a sling, a few stones, and an unwavering faith in God, David killed Goliath with one, well-planted shot (vv. 12–49). Following this heroic act, David was exalted by the people of Israel. The women even sang, " 'Saul has slain his thousands, / And David his ten thousands' " (18:7). This attention paid to David enraged Saul and made him suspicious of the young boy (vv. 8–9). Indeed, the day following Saul's triumphant return to Jerusalem, he tried to kill David (vv. 10–11). Some time later, David had to flee from Saul's presence and remain on the run because Saul vehemently sought to take his life. The ordeal did not end until Saul committed suicide after being badly wounded in battle (18:28–31:6). During this terrible period in David's life, he found a close friend in Saul's son, Jonathan. The biblical text records that "the soul of Jonathan was knit to the soul of David, and Jonathan loved him as himself" (18:1b). Regardless of his father's open hatred of David, Jonathan never betrayed his friendship with David. Jonathan repeatedly encouraged his companion and protected him from Saul's wrath.

> **Principle Three**
> Companions take our part when others try to take us apart.

IV. A Song for the Lonely to Sing

In the 1960s and early 1970s, the United States was being ripped apart by factions that were divided over the Vietnam War. During those tumultuous years, Paul Simon composed some poignant lyrics and put them to music. One song that he wrote reassured millions of people that when everything falls down around them, one thing will get them through—a friend. The second verse of that beautiful song gives a message we all can sing:

> When you're down and out, when you're on the street,
> When evening falls so hard, I will comfort you.
> I'll take your part.
>
> Oh! When darkness comes and pain is all around,
> Like a bridge over troubled water, I will lay me down.[1]

We cannot make it through days of disillusionment and times of trouble without friends. One plus one *does* equal survival.

Living Insights

Study One

This passage instructs us on the advantages of having a real friend. Let's turn our attention to a touching example of companionship from the historical section of the Old Testament.

● Tucked away between Judges and 1 Samuel is the tiny book of Ruth. After you make a copy of the following chart, read through the four brief chapters of Ruth, giving close attention to principles of friendship from its story. Jot them down in personal terms so they relate to *you*.

---

1. "Bridge Over Troubled Water." Words and music by Paul Simon, 1969.

Ruth and Naomi: True Friends	
Principles of Friendship	References

Living Insights

As you read about Ruth and Naomi, can you identify a similar friendship in your life? It's a special friendship, isn't it? Let's concentrate on some concrete ways to honor that companion.

- How do you show your appreciation to your closest friend? Here are three suggestions:
  1. Express your gratitude verbally or in writing.
  2. Show your appreciation with a gift, a favor, or some other demonstrative act of kindness.
  3. Pray for your friend. Thank God for the influence of his/her life on you, and pray for any requests of which you are aware.

What Every Worshiper Should Remember

Ecclesiastes 5:1–7

Much of Solomon's journal is filled with horizontal musings on the barrenness of life. But on a few occasions, his diary is punctuated with vertical insights that scrape away the veneer of empty religion and drive us back to a meaningful relationship with God. The opening verses of Ecclesiastes 5 provide one of these rare moments. Like a cool oasis in the middle of a hot, dry desert, these seven verses allow the Christian an opportunity to take an honest look at his worship of, and walk with, the living God. They do not complicate the issue with incomprehensible jargon and complex techniques. Instead, Solomon's words get down to the basics of a believer's devotion to God. Let's fix our attention on the directives he gives.

I. The Word of God: Hope for Our Times

From time to time, we need to be reminded that the Bible provides the only infallible written counsel on how to connect with the Lord in a meaningful way. On the foundations of relating to God, the Scriptures have both brilliance and simplicity—rare qualities in a world marked by complexity and confusion. Among the biblical writers, the author of Hebrews most succinctly expresses the relevance and power of God's Word. Here's what he says: "For the Word of God is living and active and sharper than any two-edged sword, and piercing as far as the division of soul and spirit, of both joints and marrow, and able to judge the thoughts and intentions of the heart. And there is no creature hidden from His sight, but all things are open and laid bare to the eyes of Him with whom we have to do" (Heb. 4:12–13). These words relate to some of Scripture's functions and convey two reasons why the Bible is effective.

A. What God's Word does (v. 12). First, the Bible *pierces*. It cuts through the excuses we give, the rationalizations we manufacture, and the barriers we raise. This leads to the second activity God's Word performs—*judgment*. The Bible exposes the truth about even our innermost thoughts and motivations. It leaves nothing in our lives untouched.

B. Why God's Word works (v. 13). Why is it that the Bible remains relevant to all—regardless of sex, age, circumstance, location, culture, or era? The first reason is that it is *universal in scope*. No creature can hide from Scripture's divine Author and penetrating truths. The second reason is that it is *limitless in its exposure*. The Greek word for *open* means "uncovered," and the term translated *laid bare* comes from the Greek word from which we get our English word *trachea*. Some background information will help us understand the meaning of *laid bare*. When an animal was sacrificed during the first century, its head was raised so that its throat would be exposed. Then the priest would plunge his knife deep into the animal's throat and draw out its blood for the sacrifice. In other terms, when God's Word lays our lives bare, it goes for the jugular. And since we always need the great Physician's touch, we always find His Word—the printed scalpel—cutting into our lives so that we can experience His healing power.

II. The Worship of God: Truth for Our Minds

In Ecclesiastes 5:1–7a, Solomon's journal turns from the secular to the religious, from the sphere of work to the realm of worship. The Preacher does not mince words; he jumps right into his subject without any transition. In fact, his first words form a strong exhortation, a sentinel-like declaration: "Guard your steps as you go to the house of God" (Eccles. 5:1a). When we enter into God's presence, we are not to be dull-minded or insensitive, but we are to stay alert and attentive. After all, worship ushers us spiritually into the throne room of the living, all-righteous Lord. Even His children dare not take this fact lightly. Following this general exhortation, Solomon unfolds four commands and gives corresponding reasons for obeying them. Each is designed to guide and encourage us in our worship of the sovereign King.

A. **Draw near and listen well, because God is communicating** (v. 1b). Solomon says, "Draw near to listen rather than to offer the sacrifice of fools; for they do not know they are doing evil." The phrase "sacrifice of fools" probably refers to fruitless and irrelevant talk (cf. vv. 2–3, 7; 1 Kings 18:25–29, Matt. 6:7). Solomon is telling us to close our mouths and open our ears as we prepare for worship. God speaks to us through the music, prayer, and sermon. But we will not hear Him if our vocal cords are working overtime.

B. **Be quiet and stay calm, because God hears the inaudible and sees the invisible** (vv. 2–3, 7a). Observe what Solomon says in Ecclesiastes 5 regarding this: "Do not be hasty in word or impulsive in thought to bring up a matter in the presence of God. For God is in heaven and you are on the earth; therefore let your words be few. For the dream comes through much effort, and the voice of a fool through many words. . . . For in many dreams and in many words there is emptiness." Old Testament exegete Derek Kidner explains an essential element in this command: "The dreams appear to be daydreams, reducing worship to verbal [or mental] doodling."[1]

Derek Kidner, *The Message of Ecclesiastes* (Downers Grove: InterVarsity Press, 1976), p. 53.

It is all too easy for us to let our minds wander from one scene to another. We may begin thinking about a recent day of recreation at the lake, upcoming demands to be met at the office, the stack of clothes at home that need washing and ironing, or anything else. Solomon's exhortation to us is: Don't daydream; stop churning; be calm. Psalm 46:10a expresses this thought well when it says, " 'Cease striving and know that I am God.' " We need to let go of our concerns, anxieties, and preoccupations when we enter into the Lord's presence. We are commanded to do this not simply so we can hear God and know Him better, but also because He hears our inner thoughts as well as our spoken words. His heavenly perspective enables Him to penetrate and expose all that we think, say, and do. So we need to guard our actions, words, and thoughts and listen attentively to what the Lord has to say to us.

C. **Make a commitment and keep it, because God accepts it and doesn't forget it** (vv. 4–5). The Preacher's point in Ecclesiastes 5 is clear on this: "When you make a vow to God, do not be late in paying it, for He takes no delight in fools. Pay what you vow! It is better that you should not vow than that you should vow and not pay." In our day of empty promises and shallow commitments, we need to heed these words. We should never make a vow to God that we do not plan to keep. And when we do make an oath, we should carry it out fully, for the Lord takes our vows seriously (1 Sam. 1:9–2:11).

D. **Don't decide now and deny later, because God doesn't ignore decisions** (v. 6). This verse from Ecclesiastes 5 comes on the heels of the command to fulfill our commitments to God. Here Solomon adds some strong words: "Do not let your speech cause you to sin and do not say in the presence of the messenger of God that it was a mistake. Why should God be angry on account of your voice and destroy the work of your hands?" If we were to restate the essence of this passage in the vernacular of our day, it might sound like this: Don't try to worm out of a decision you have made before God. Such an act will lead to sin and God's discipline. As the Lord said to Israel in Moses' day, " 'When you make a vow to the Lord your God, you shall not delay to pay it, for it would be sin in you, and the Lord your God will surely require it of you' " (Deut. 23:21).

III. The Warning of God: Strength for Our Lives

Solomon wraps up his instruction concerning worship with a solemn warning: "Fear God" (Eccles. 5:7b). We are to take God seriously. We should never play games with the Creator and Sustainer of th universe. He demands our utmost respect and diligent obedience; nothing short of this will do. Regarding this fact, David Allan Hubbard's words ring loud and true:

> Better to bribe a judge than to ply God with hollow words; better to slap a policeman than to seek God's influence by meaningless gestures; better to perjure yourself in court than to harry God with promises you cannot keep. The full adorations of our spirit, the true obedience of our heart—these are his demands and his delights.[2]

Living Insights

Study One

Worship should not be a passive experience. Solomon speaks out strongly about this. His goal is to show us that worship should be alive, active, and vibrant. After all, that's the way God intended it!

- The following chart contains some of the action words from Ecclesiastes 5:1–7. Copy the chart into your notebook and begin researching the words. Start by writing down terms that are *opposite* in meaning to each particular word listed below. Often contrasts broaden our understanding. Then write down a statement addressing *why* each word is important.

An Active Worshiper—Ecclesiastes 5:1–7		
Action Words	Contrasting Words	Importance of Words
Guard		
Draw Near		
Listen		
Hasty in Word		
Impulsive in Thought		
Dream		
Make a Vow		
Pay		
Speech		
Sin		
Destroy		
Fear		

. David Allan Hubbard, *Beyond Futility* (Grand Rapids: William B. Eerdmans Publishing Co., 1976), p. 71.

⚘ Living Insights

Have you ever thought about what worship was like in Old Testament times? The Book of Leviticus has much to say about this very subject. Another book worth consulting is the hymnal which was used in conjunction with worship in the Temple. This work is known to us today as the Book of Psalms.

- Let's worship the Lord through our songs of praise. Grab a hymnbook and pick out some favorites. Better yet, look for those hymns that have their words rooted in the Psalms themselves. Close your eyes and imagine you are in the Temple worshiping God in Old Testament Jerusalem, just as Solomon did so long ago. Keep in mind the points we covered in this study as you worship God in song.

⚒ Digging Deeper

The subject of vows raises the question as to whether Jesus sanctioned or condemned the practice of oath-taking when He spoke these words:

> "Again, you have heard that the ancients were told, 'You shall not make false vows, but shall fulfill your vows to the Lord.' But I say to you, make no oath at all, either by heaven, for it is the throne of God, or by the earth, for it is the footstool of His feet, or by Jerusalem, for it is the city of the Great King. Nor shall you make an oath by your head, for you cannot make one hair white or black. But let your statement be, 'Yes, yes' or 'No, no'; and anything beyond these is of evil." (Matt. 5:33–37)

Some people maintain that Jesus sought to abolish the making of all vows. But this position would place Christ in opposition to the Old Testament—a body of teaching that He was sent to uphold and fulfill, not undermine and contradict (vv. 17–19). In addition, this interpretation of the Lord's statements would put Him at odds with His own practice, for He swore an oath before Caiaphas, the high priest, that He was " 'the Christ, the Son of God' " (26:63–64). This understanding would also contradict affirmations given elsewhere in the New Testament regarding oaths made by both God and man (see Heb. 6:13–18). How, then, should we interpret Christ's statements about vow-making? We should understand His teaching as a challenge to a widespread rabbinic tradition that violated and softened the Old Testament instruction on oaths. During Jesus' day, it was taught that the only vows which were binding were those made directly to God or spoken in His name. Thus, swearing by heaven, by the earth, by Jerusalem, by the hairs on one's head, or by any other thing became a means to renege on a promise without violating the Law. Chris exposed the fallacy in this reasoning by pointing out that heaven is God's throne, earth His footstool, Jerusalem His city, and one's head God's possession (Matt. 5:34–36). Therefore, any oath made to God, given in His name, or spoken in regard to any part of His creation is morally binding. Beyond this, Jesus commanded that everything we say be truthful and dependable, for anything less is evil (v. 37). If you desire to learn more about the scriptural teaching on vows, then we recommend that you consult the Scripture passages and study aids listed below.

- **Some Pertinent Biblical Passages**
  Principles Regarding Vow-Making: Leviticus 5:4–6, 19:12, 22:21–23; Numbers 6:1–21, 30:1–16; Deuteronomy 6:13–15, 10:20, 23:21–23; Psalms 15:4, 24:4–5, 76:11, 89:30–37; Proverbs 20:25; Ecclesiastes 5:4–5; Zechariah 5:3–4; Matthew 5:33–37, 23:16–22; James 5:12

  Examples of Vow-Making: Genesis 14:21–24, 21:22–24, 24:1–67, 25:27–34, 28:20–22, 31:4–18, 47:29–31, 50:4–6, 24–26; Exodus 13:18–19, 32:11–14; Leviticus 27:1–33; Numbers 5:19–28, 6:1–21, 15:1–10, 21:1–3; Deuteronomy 12:10–18, 34:1–4; Joshua 2:1–21, 14:6–13, 23:6–8; Judges 11:29–40, 15:9–13; Ruth 1:16–18; 1 Samuel 1:9–2:11, 20:1–42, 24:17–22, 28:3–25, 30:11–20; 2 Samuel 3:31–37, 15:7–12, 19:5–7; 1 Kings 1:28–31, 51–52, 2:36–46; 2 Chronicles 36:11–21; Nehemiah 9:15, 13:23–29; Psalms 22:25, 50:14, 56:12, 61:5–8, 63:11, 66:13, 95:8–11, 119:106, 110:4, 116:12–19, 132:1–18; Proverbs 7:14, 31:2; Isaiah 19:19–22, 45:22–25, 48:1–11, 54:9, 62:6–9; Jeremiah 4:1–2, 5:1–3, 7:8–11, 12:16–17, 22:5, 32:21–22, 38:14–28, 44:24–28; Ezekiel 20:5–44; Amos 4:2, 6:8–11, 8:14; Jonah 1:16, 2:9; Micah 7:19–20; Zephaniah 1:4–6; Malachi 1:10–14, 3:5–6; Matthew 14:1–12, 26:63–64, 69–75; Luke 1:67–75; Acts 2:29–32, 18:18, 21:22–26; Romans 9:1–2; 2 Corinthians 1:23; Hebrews 3:16–19, 6:13–18, 7:17–22; Revelation 10:4–7

- **Some Helpful Study Aids**
  Gehman, Henry Snyder, ed. "Vow." In *The New Westminster Dictionary of the Bible,* pp. 984–85. Philadelphia: The Westminster Press, 1970.

  MacArthur, John F., Jr. *Matthew 1–7.* The MacArthur New Testament Commentary Series, pp. 320–26. Chicago: Moody Press, 1985.

  Masselink, William. "Vow." In *Evangelical Dictionary of Theology,* edited by Walter A. Elwell, pp. 1148–49. Grand Rapids: Baker Book House, 1984.

  Unger, Merrill F. "Vow." In *Unger's Bible Dictionary,* rev. ed., pp. 1159–60. Chicago: Moody Press, 1966.

Straight Talk to the Money-Mad
Ecclesiastes 5:8–20

Centuries ago, a famous queen paid a visit to a very rich king. She had heard reports about his immense wealth, infallible wisdom, political skills, architectural accomplishments, musical talents, and religious commitment. But she suspected that the accounts of his fame had been exaggerated. So, with heightened curiosity, she went to Jerusalem to meet this royal figure and see for herself if the testimonies were true. The biblical text records that "when the queen of Sheba perceived all the wisdom of [King] Solomon, the house that he had built, the food of his table, the seating of his servants, the attendance of his waiters and their attire, his cupbearers, and his stairway by which he went up to the house of the Lord, there was no more spirit in her" (1 Kings 10:4–5). Astounded by what she had witnessed, the queen confessed to Solomon, " 'It was a true report which I heard in my own land about your words and your wisdom. Nevertheless I did not believe the reports, until I came and my eyes had seen it. And behold, *the half was not told me.* You exceed in wisdom and prosperity the report which I heard' " (vv. 6–7, emphasis added). To this testimony, the Bible adds, "King Solomon became greater than all the kings of the earth in riches and in wisdom. And all the earth was seeking the presence of Solomon, to hear his wisdom which God had put in his heart" (vv. 23–24). Wouldn't it be great if we could glean Solomon's experienced perspective on the pursuit of affluence? And indeed we can, by examining what he says in Ecclesiastes 5:8–20. Here he tells us some of what he learned about money and its abuse by the money-mad. The results are insightful observations and relevant counsel that every generation would be wise to consider. Let's do that for ourselves right now.

I. Proverbial Principles to Learn
Written between the lines of Ecclesiastes 5:8–12, we find three proverbs that relate directly to finances.

A. The rich tend to take charge, and their power intimidates and offends the poor. This truth grows out of Solomon's observation of the world: "If you see oppression of the poor and denial of justice and righteousness in the province, do not be shocked at the sight, for one official watches over [or protects] another official, and there are higher officials over them" (v. 8). An abundance of money frequently brings its possessors a greater degree of power and prestige. And this often leads to their gaining control of more money, land, and enterprises. Many times, wealth will even help place individuals in political offices where they can establish laws that favor their own economic advancement. In situations like this, the rich get richer and the poor get poorer. The greater the chasm between

the classes becomes, the harder it is for the poor to gain an audience with the rich. In fact, the well-to-do frequently erect a hierarchy of officials that make it virtually impossible for the down-and-out to get fair treatment. The end result is too often the corruption of justice and the oppression of the poor. Does this mean that leadership should be abolished and money equally distributed? Not in the least! What this passage does suggest is that the rich—especially those who are civic leaders—should use their wealth and power compassionately, not oppressively. King Solomon says as much when he writes, "A king who [wisely] cultivates the field is an advantage to the land" (v. 9).

B. Greed and materialism have no built-in safeguards or satisfying limits. Solomon probably had more opportunities to obtain contentment through the pursuit and achievement of affluence than anyone else who has ever lived. And yet, he concluded that the love of money, possessions, or both will never satisfy. Consider his words: "He who loves money will not be satisfied with money, nor he who loves abundance with its income. This too is vanity" (v. 10). It should be observed that this verse is *not* an attack on those who possess riches. Rather, this passage is a direct assault on the money-hungry who greedily strive for more. People like this will never have enough, and therefore, will always be dissatisfied. In addition, they will eventually harm themselves and fall under the righteous judgment of God (Luke 12:13–21, 16:19–31; 1 Tim. 6:9–10, James 5:1–6).

C. With increased money and possessions comes an accelerated number of people and worries. Solomon vividly depicts this truth with two observations. The first is this: "When good things increase, those who consume them increase. So what is the advantage to their owners except to look on?" (Eccles. 5:11). As individuals grow wealthier, they usually find themselves surrounded by an entourage of people who draw pay from their riches. A contemporary writer described this phenomenon rather bluntly: "When man's possessions increase, it seems there's a corresponding increase in the number of parasites who live off him: Management consultants, tax advisers, accountants, lawyers, household employees, and sponging relatives."[1] More money also brings more anxiety. Questions arise in the minds of the rich that were not quite as troubling when there was less money to manage. Worries over whether certain deals are going to pay off or fall through, or whether

1. William McDonald, *Chasing the Wind* (Chicago: Moody Press, 1975), p. 47.

employees are earning their keep or stealing from the till, constantly plague the well-to-do. The result of such struggles is often sleepless nights. This is the second observation Solomon makes: "The sleep of the working man is pleasant, whether he eats little or much. But the full stomach of the rich man does not allow him to sleep" (v. 12). In short, Solomon is saying this: More money, more people; more people, more worries; more worries, less sleep. From the outside, the life of the rich may seem delightful, satisfying, and carefree. But on the inside, it is frequently marked by frustration, discontentment, anxiety, and loneliness.

II. Grievous Evils to Remember

In Ecclesiastes 5:13–17, Solomon reminds us of two evils riches can bring. As we examine what he says, we should recall that he is rightly condemning the insatiable pursuit of wealth, not wealth itself.

A. Those who have clutched can quickly crash. Notice what the Israelite king observed:

> There is a grievous evil which I have seen under the sun: riches being hoarded by their owner to his hurt. When those riches were lost through a bad investment and he had fathered a son, then there was nothing to support him. As he had come naked from his mother's womb, so will he return as he came. He will take nothing from the fruit of his labor that he can carry in his hand. (vv. 13–15)

Our material possessions will not be ours forever. It makes no difference how tightly we hang on to them. We will either lose them during this life or leave them behind when we pass on. There are no other alternatives.

B. Those who live high often die hard. "Exactly as a man is born, thus will he die. So, what is the advantage to him who toils for the wind? Throughout his life he also eats in darkness with great vexation, sickness and anger" (vv. 16b–17). What a despairing scene! The touch-me-not, I've-got-it-made materialist who lives in earthly opulence is not as well off as he or she might seem. Such people soon discover that money cannot buy happiness, contentment, or peace. In fact, their insatiable drive for wealth usually fills their lives with futility, resentment, and pain, the end of which is a lonely death and a cold grave.

III. Good and Fitting Gifts to Claim

In Ecclesiastes 5:18–20, Solomon lifts the cloud of despair and doom that settles over the money-mad and exposes the light of satisfaction and grace that shines on the money-sane. Here, he reveals three

God-given gifts that are available for us to claim and savor if we possess God's perspective on wealth.

A. Claim the gift of enjoyment in your life. Solomon writes that it is "good and fitting . . . to eat, to drink and enjoy oneself in all one's labor in which he toils under the sun during the few years of his life which God has given him; for this is his reward" (v. 18). As we live out our lives, we need to find pleasure in our activities. But this can only happen if we refuse to commit ourselves to the pursuit of possessions.

B. Claim the gift of fulfillment in your work. "As for every man to whom God has given riches and wealth, He has also empowered him to eat from them and to receive his reward and rejoice in his labor; this is the gift of God" (v. 19). Fulfillment can be found in our present work. But many of us don't discover it because we are busy dreaming of a better job, dissatisfied with what we have. One problem with this kind of thinking is that the grass is not always greener on the other side of the fence. So rather than constantly hoping for something better that may never come, we ought to seek gratification in what we do now. And when we engage in our work with service to God as the goal, personal satisfaction will be ours.

C. Claim the gift of contentment in your heart. One who is fulfilled in his work "will not often consider the years of his life, because God keeps him occupied with the gladness of his heart" (v. 20). We can experience inner peace and joy as we focus on the Lord and revel in His provisions, whether they be adequate or abundant. On the other hand, if we are money-hungry, we will never find happiness and rest. Money cannot buy contentment. Satisfaction is a gift of God.

Living Insights

Study One ■■■■■■■■■■■■■■■■■■■■■■■■■■■■■■■■■■

One of the most popular misquotes from Scripture is, "Money is the root of all evil." First Timothy 6:10 actually says that "the *love* of money is a root of all sorts of evil" (emphasis added). There are other misconceptions about riches. Many well-meaning Christians have put forth mistaken ideas about money with little or no scriptural support.

● With the help of a Bible concordance, let's check out the references in Scripture to *money, rich, riches, wealth,* and *wealthy.* Jot down the references on your copy of the following chart. Then, summarize their teaching in the right-hand column.

Biblical References to Riches	
Scriptures	Summary Statements

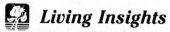

Living Insights

As a result of study one, we now have a better understanding of what Scripture says about riches. Now it's time to turn our attention to the question, "How do I view riches?"

- As you look at the following chart, you'll notice it's identical to the previous one except for an added column. What do the verses you researched in the previous study mean to you? How is your view of wealth enriched by your understanding of these texts? Use this time to personally interact with the material.

Riches and Me		
Scriptures	Summary Statements	Personal Reflections

The Few Years of a Futile Life
Ecclesiastes 6

The scenes Solomon has "painted" in his journal evoke vivid images. We could even imagine them as actual portraits hanging in a gallery with these titles attached to them:
— The Bewildered Philosopher
— The Funny-faced Clown
— The Hedonistic Playboy
— The Good-time Charlie
— The Industrious Worker
— The Oppressed Victim
— The Disillusioned Top Dog
— The Faithful Friend
— The Committed Worshiper
— The Greedy Materialist

As we continue walking through the gallery of Solomon's journal, we find still another portrait. This one bears a resemblance to those we have already viewed, and yet its differences are striking. It is painted in dark, drab colors that convey a sense of struggle, pain . . . even anguish. As we examine it more closely, we will discern that it is the self-portrait of a troubled king. He has not attached his name to it, but there is little doubt that Ecclesiastes 6 is a picture of Solomon as he sees himself. This portrait is a disturbing one, not only because of how it depicts a God-fearing leader, but also because it drives us to seriously examine our own lives. So let's prepare for a time of soul-searching as we begin our study of this haunting portrait.

I. An Enlargement of a Single Portrait

While portraying himself, Solomon presents life as it is. In doing so, he compels us to come to terms with reality. Let's explore the dimensions of this painting as the artist presents them in Ecclesiastes 6.

A. The subject and the situation. Solomon reveals the identity of the painter in verses 1–2: "There is an evil which I have seen under the sun and it is prevalent among men—a man to whom God has given riches and wealth and honor so that his soul lacks nothing of all that he desires, but God has not empowered him to eat from them, for a foreigner enjoys them. This is vanity and a severe affliction." The phrase "a man to whom God has given riches and wealth and honor" can be traced to 2 Chronicles 1:12, where God speaks to Solomon in very similar terminology: " 'I will give you riches and wealth and honor, such as none of the kings who were before you has possessed, nor those who will come after you.' " We know from the biblical record and archaeological discoveries that God fulfilled this promise to Solomon.[1] But the Lord did not grant him the ability to enjoy the benefits of his wealth and fame. Solomon does not tell us why God withheld this gift from him, but it was most likely because of his departure from a full devotion to the Lord (1 Kings 11:1–13). At any rate, Solomon does convey that the fruits of his labor are being enjoyed by "a foreigner" (Eccles. 6:2b). Although *foreigner* is not specifically defined, it could signify a personal enemy, a debilitating illness, a domestic conflict, or even a natural calamity. But whatever it is, Solomon laments the fact that the rewards he longs for are being reaped by another. It's little wonder that he describes this situation as "vanity and a severe affliction" (v. 2c).

B. A few added details. Examining this self-portrait more closely leads us to discover faint traces of bright color that are overshadowed by the dreary browns and grays. Apparently, Solomon tried to overcome his frustration and despair by adding various things to his life that had the potential of bringing him true happiness. For example, he mentions that he had *many children* in hopes of finding satisfaction. But his persistent inability to enjoy the fruit of his toil led him to conclude that it would have been better if he had been the victim of a miscarriage (v. 3). Why? Because a miscarried fetus " 'comes in futility and goes into obscurity; and its name is covered in obscurity. It never sees the sun and it never knows anything' " (vv. 4–5a). Since parenthood proves to be an inadequate solution for dissatisfaction, Solomon considers adding *more years* to one's life as a viable alternative. But he concludes that even a two-thousand-year life span would be miserable if one " 'does not enjoy good things' " (v. 6a). Besides, the person who lives only a few years and the individual who lives many years both wind up in the same place—the grave (v. 6b). So what benefit is there in living a long life? Solomon also reflects on his attempt at using *hard work* to relieve his depression. But that did not work either; his "appetite"—literally, "soul"—was "not satisfied" (v. 7). Intensified labor will not bring contentment to an empty life. Then what about a *good education and practical discernment?* Can they accomplish what the other things cannot? Again, Solomon answers no. "For what advantage does the wise man have over the fool? What advantage does the poor man have, knowing how to walk before the living?" (v. 8). There is none. The bottom line is that "what the eyes see

1. Some resources that present this information are listed in footnote 2 on page 2 of this study guide.

is better than what the soul desires" (v. 9a). We need to stop dreaming about what we don't have and be content with what we do have. Dreams can give us goals to strive for, but they cannot fill empty stomachs, pay outstanding bills, and provide lasting satisfaction. We cannot begin to discover contentment until we face reality.

C. **Some realistic observations.** As we explore the background of Solomon's portrait, we find a particular hue that is laced throughout and yet rarely draws attention to itself. Nonetheless, we need to understand what it signifies before we can fully grasp the message this painting conveys. Solomon does not leave us in doubt concerning the thoughts this color symbolizes. He gives them to us in verses 10–11.

1. **God is sovereign.** Solomon states that "whatever exists has already been named" (v. 10a). In Scripture, the act of naming something is a sign of sovereignty over that thing. For instance, when Adam gave names to all the animals, he was exercising his God-given right and responsibility to rule over the earth (Gen. 2:19–20; cf. 1:26–28). However, God has named man, each of the stars, and everything else that was not placed under man's rule (5:2, Ps. 147:4, Eccles. 6:10a). Therefore, the Lord is the King over all of creation. As a result, everything is under His perfect, all-knowing control; nothing that happens takes Him by surprise or causes Him to modify His plan (cf. Gen. 45:4–8, 50:19–20; Job 14:5; Ps. 2; Dan. 2:20–23, 4:17; Acts 4:27–28). Of course, we might doubt God's sovereignty when a "foreigner" invades our lives and robs us of joy. But then we must rest in the fact that "God causes all things to work together for good to those who love God, to those who are called according to His purpose" (Rom. 8:28).

2. **Mankind is not sovereign.** Solomon puts it in these terms: "It is known what man is" (Eccles. 6:10b). The evidence is abundant and clear. Man is inconsistent, weak, unfaithful, and limited in knowledge. The Lord, on the other hand, is consistent, mighty, faithful, and all-knowing. Furthermore, as a consequence of his sin, man has temporarily lost his delegated sovereignty over the earth (Gen. 3:16–19, Heb. 2:6–8). And although his dominion will be restored one day, he will never reign over the entire creation but will be in submission to God's authority forever (Rev. 21–22).

3. **Disputing with God is a waste of time and effort.** As Solomon says, "He [man] cannot dispute with him who is stronger than he is. For there are many words which

increase futility. What then is the advantage to a man?" (Eccles. 6:10c–11). There is none. In fact, quarreling with the Creator can bring discipline and even judgment. The prophet Isaiah states as much when he writes these words of warning:

> "Woe to the one who quarrels with his Maker—An earthenware vessel among the vessels of earth!
> Will the clay say to the potter, 'What are you doing?'
> Or the thing you are making say, 'He has no hands'?
> Woe to him who says to a father, 'What are you begetting?'
> Or to a woman, 'To what are you giving birth?' "
> Thus says the Lord, the Holy One of Israel, and his Maker:
> "Ask Me about the things to come concerning My sons,
> And you shall commit to Me the work of My hands.
> It is I who made the earth, and created man upon it.
> I stretched out the heavens with My hands,
> And I ordained all their host." (Isa. 45:9–12)

Clearly, arguing with God is a waste of our time. He always operates according to His will. The Book of Daniel leaves no doubt concerning this fact:

> "For His dominion is an everlasting dominion,
> And His kingdom endures from generation to generation.
> And all the inhabitants of the earth are accounted as nothing,
> But He does according to His will in the host of heaven
> And among the inhabitants of earth;
> And no one can ward off His hand
> Or say to Him, 'What hast Thou done?' "
> (Dan. 4:34b–35)

II. A Look at Our Own Portrait

The words that put the final touches on Solomon's self-portrait prompt us to take a close look at ourselves. Let's read his closing statement and then ponder the questions it raises. Solomon writes "Who knows what is good for a man during his lifetime, during the few years of his futile life? He will spend them like a shadow. For who can tell a man what will be after him under the sun?" (Eccles. 6:12).

A. Does life seem futile? More than likely, it does to all of us at times. And when we become frustrated, bewildered, and discontent, we often dispute with God. Fortunately, He graciously tolerates our contentious spirits and lovingly seeks to persuade us to stop fighting Him and start trusting Him. Will you do that?

B. Are you fearful about the future? None of us knows what our future holds. The very fact that even our best laid plans frequently have to be revised—if not abandoned—is ample proof of this (James 4:13–15). However, Jesus Christ has assured us that if we build our lives on His Word and act on His counsel, then we will be " 'compared to a wise man, who built his house upon the rock. And the rain descended, and the floods came, and the winds blew, and burst against that house; and yet it did not fall, for it had been founded upon the rock' " (Matt. 7:24–25). On the other hand, if we hear His Word and fail to order our lives after it, then we " 'will be like a foolish man, who built his house upon the sand. And the rain descended, and the floods came, and the winds blew, and burst against that house; and it fell, and great was its fall' " (vv. 26–27). On which foundation does your life rest—rock or sand? The answer to this question will reveal your ultimate destiny—heaven or hell.

Living Insights

Study One

Ecclesiastes 6 . . . twelve verses on futility. Behind the words are feelings of frustration and discontentment. Let's dig deeper into this chapter in order to further identify with Solomon's feelings.

● One of the finest ways to personally interact with the Scriptures is to study the verses and write them down *in your own words*. This is known as *paraphrasing*. It's a great way to get down to the feelings and attitudes expressed on the pages. Put yourself in Solomon's place in order to visualize the futility described in Ecclesiastes 6.

🌿 Living Insights

The first phrase of Ecclesiastes 6:9 is fascinating: "What the eyes see is better than what the soul desires." These words seem to contrast *realism* and *idealism*—what the eyes see and what the soul desires. How does this apply to you? Are you a realist? An idealist? Or, most likely, a mixture of both? With the help of the following charts, do a little self-assessment on your attitude toward life.

The Realist inside Me
In what areas of my life do I tend toward realism?
What are the advantages of this realism?
What are the disadvantages?

The Idealist inside Me
In what areas of my life do I tend toward idealism?
What are the advantages of this idealism?
What are the disadvantages?

Wise Words for Busy People
Ecclesiastes 7:1–14

At some point in our lives, we all have contact with a rebel—one who defiantly goes his or her way even if it contradicts reason and experience. The rebel we know may be an employer, a parent, a friend, a spouse—or perhaps it is ourselves. But whoever it is, we can be confident that one who rebels against God—whether that person is a believer or not—is turning away from the Giver of wisdom who provides solid advice for handling life (cf. Prov. 8:1–9:6, James 1:5). King Solomon learned this truth the hard way. Rather than heed God's command not to associate with foreign women, Solomon disobeyed by marrying many non-Israelites who eventually turned his devotion away from the Lord. Apparently, it was during this period of defiance that Solomon sought to find satisfaction on a purely human level. The consequences of this rebellion were serious. God disciplined him by raising up foreign adversaries who brought much turmoil to his final years as Israel's ruler (1 Kings 11). And, as Solomon has recorded in Ecclesiastes, his search for happiness under the sun uncovered only vanity and despair. His findings are summarized in these words: "So I hated life, for the work which had been done under the sun was grievous to me; because everything is futility and striving after wind. Thus I hated all the fruit of my labor for which I had labored under the sun" (Eccles. 2:17–18a). Fortunately, Solomon's outlook did not remain on a horizontal plane. The emptiness he discovered caused him to look up. And although we have already seen glimpses of his change in perspective, we will find more evidences of it in the latter half of his journal. The benefit for us is some divinely inspired counsel from a former rebel that can revolutionize our lives for the better.

I. A Change in Scenery
In the first six chapters of Ecclesiastes, Solomon describes human existence—ragged-edge reality—without God. However, from chapter 7 on, his focus becomes less man-centered and more God-centered. His journey away from the Lord is ending; he is beginning to come back home. Some evidence of this change is the frequent occurrence of two terms, *wise* and *wisdom*. They appear almost thirty-five times in the latter half of his journal. Furthermore, the seventh chapter opens with several proverbs that offer a godly perspective on dealing with life. So that we may better understand the proverbs Solomon gives, let's take this opportunity to survey three types that appear in the Bible.

A. Contrastive couplets.
Proverbs that fall under this category are composed of two parts that are usually connected with the terms *but* or *nevertheless*. Here are some examples:

> A wise son accepts his father's discipline,
> But a scoffer does not listen to rebuke.
>> (Prov. 13:1)
> Through presumption comes nothing but strife,
> But with those who receive counsel is wisdom.
>> (v. 10)

B. Completive couplets. This type of proverb brings two similar or parallel thoughts together with the words *and* or *so*. The following are representative of this category:

> The heart knows its own bitterness,
> And a stranger does not share its joy.
>> (14:10)
> Even in laughter the heart may be in pain,
> And the end of joy may be grief.
>> (v. 13)

C. Comparative couplets. These proverbs link two ideas with the terms *better/than* or *like/so*. The examples below illustrate this variety:

> It is better to live in a corner of the roof
> Than in a house shared with a contentious woman.
>> (25:24)
> Like cold water to a weary soul,
> So is good news from a distant land.
>> (v. 25)

II. Counsel for Those in the Crunch

In Ecclesiastes 7:1–10, Solomon sets forth a number of proverbs—seven comparative, one contrastive (v. 4), and another completive (v. 7). Let's consider each one. While we do, we will hear some of the counsel that marked Solomon's pilgrimage back to God. At the same time, we will glean some guidance for our own journey through life.

A. "A good name is better than a good ointment" (v. 1a). The Hebrew term for *ointment* might be better rendered *perfume* or *cologne*. The principle here is that an excellent reputation is more valuable than any pleasant-smelling fragrance we might apply (1 Pet. 3:3–4). Our physical impression on others is not unimportant, but it is certainly less important than our character and integrity.

B. "The day of one's death is better than the day of one's birth" (v. 1b). This wise saying from Ecclesiastes 7 may sound pessimistic, but it need not be understood in this way. Why? Because death can be considered a victory. The Apostle Paul expressed a similar viewpoint when he wrote these words:

> For to me, to live is Christ and to die is gain. But if
> I am to live on in the flesh, this will mean fruitful
> labor for me; and I do not know which to choose.
> But I am hard-pressed from both directions, having
> the desire to depart and be with Christ, for that is
> very much better; yet to remain on in the flesh is
> more necessary for your sake. (Phil. 1:21–24)

For those of us who are believers, the joyous forever following our death will be better than even the happy days that followed our birth.

C. **"It is better to go to a house of mourning / Than to go to a house of feasting"** (v. 2). This verse in Ecclesiastes 7 prods us to consider death, and thereby, move beyond the superficial and on to the significant matters of life. In doing so, we take a crucial step toward living wisely.

D. **"Sorrow is better than laughter. . . ."** (vv. 3–4). In these verses Solomon is not advocating that we trudge through life with tears in our eyes and frowns on our faces. Rather, he is advising us to soberly reflect on the brevity and destiny of our lives. This exercise can lead to a lifestyle marked by wisdom and satisfaction (cf. Ps. 90:10–17). On the other hand, those who refuse to deal with death, and who live their lives pursuing pleasure, are foolish (Eccles. 7:4b).

E. **"It is better to listen to the rebuke of a wise man / Than for one to listen to the song of fools. . . ."** (vv. 5–7). What does a fool sound like? Solomon tells us: "For as the crackling of thorn bushes [burning] under a pot, / So is the laughter of the fool, / And this too is futility" (v. 6). Fools are often fun to be with, but their entertainment-oriented lifestyle is empty. The wise, however, can sometimes seem harsh and unloving when they urge us to face reality. But as Solomon has written in the Book of Proverbs, "Faithful are the wounds of a friend, / But deceitful are the kisses of an enemy" (Prov. 27:6; cf. vv. 9, 17). Heeding the warnings and corrections of the wise is better than listening to the songs and jokes of fools. And yet, we need to be careful regarding whose counsel we follow. For even a discerning individual can succumb to the pressures of adversity or be tempted by the promise of prosperity (Eccles. 7:7).

F. **"The end of a matter is better than its beginning"** (v. 8a). Why? Because when the end is reached, the whole picture comes into view. Dreams may abound at the beginning, but reality is what's left at the end. And that's what is most important when we reach the end of our earthly lives. What we did, not what we thought about doing, is all that will count in eternity.

G. "Patience of spirit is better than haughtiness of spirit. . . ." (vv. 8b–10). On this journey from birth to death and beyond, one of God's greatest desires is the development of our character. The achievement of this objective involves replacing our pride with patience. Haughtiness tends to push wisdom aside, while forbearance can encourage its development. Solomon adds to this observation that impatience can lead to the harboring of anger and resentment—characteristics of a fool (v. 9) In addition, pride and bitterness can encourage wasteful and foolish longings for yesterday (v. 10). Wisdom, on the other hand, learns from the past, lives in the present, and looks forward to the future. As a result, the wise can flourish in the midst of gut-wrenching reality, while the foolish are dying on the ragged edge.

III. What Makes Wisdom Special

Solomon's numerous comparisons of wisdom and folly might prompt one to ask, What's so special about wisdom? Why not allow our emotions and passions to run wild? After all, don't both the wise and the foolish end up the same—dead? Solomon seems to anticipate this line of inquiry in verses 11–14 of Ecclesiastes 7. Here, he points out two major benefits of wisdom.

A. Wisdom preserves our lives from human pitfalls (vv. 11–12). Sound instruction and practical insight can help us avoid such traps as pride, impatience, disillusionment, and resentment. But it can do more than just protect us.

B. Wisdom provides our lives with divine perspective (vv. 13–14). It exhorts us to "consider the work of God." For as we do, we will realize that no one can "straighten what He has bent." The Lord is in control. Therefore, we can replace resistance and frustration with submission and relief. Indeed, trusting in God's sovereignty frees us to really enjoy the prosperity He brings and to seriously consider the adversity He permits. To this fact Solomon adds that the Lord is ultimately responsible for both the good times and the bad. He also tells us that God works through both in such a way that man cannot "discover anything that will be after him" unless God reveals it to him. In short, wisdom gives us a divine outlook that helps us rejoice in our bright days and persevere through our dark times.

IV. Some Concluding Counsel for All

There are two thoughts that we should ponder before we turn our attention away from Solomon's timeless advice.

A. We dare not make a major decision without asking for the wisdom of God.

B. We cannot see the whole picture without drawing upon the wisdom of God.

🎋 Living Insights

Solomon turns to the use of proverbial sayings in Ecclesiastes 7 and reminds us of his poetic style in his earlier writing, the Book of Proverbs. Using the comparative style, he suggests things that are "better than" other things. The obvious question this raises is *why?* Take a few minutes to copy down the following questions, and try your hand at answering them.

• Why is a good name better than a good perfume?
• Why is one's deathday better than one's birthday?
• Why is a visit to a funeral parlor better than gorging at a great feast?
• Why is sorrow better than laughter?
• Why is listening to a wise person's rebuke better than listening to a fool's song?
• Why is the end of a matter better than its beginning?
• Why is a patient spirit better than a haughty spirit?
• Why is wisdom so great?

🎋 Living Insights

"Consider the work of God, / For who is able to straighten what He has bent? / In the day of prosperity be happy / But in the day of adversity consider—/ God has made one as well as the other" (Eccles. 7:13–14a). Using this passage as a springboard, let's take a look at our lives . . . at both the days of prosperity and the days of adversity.

• Take a few minutes to reflect on the blessings that have come to you through prosperity. Make a mental list, and one by one, give thanks to God for His gracious provisions in your life.

• Now take some time to recall the blessings you have received through adversity. Remember, God made the one as well as the other. As you make a list in your mind, thank the Lord for these particular aspects of His grace in your life.

Putting Wisdom to Work
Ecclesiastes 7:15–29

It is easy for us to forget that God holds the whole world in His hands. And when we fail to live in the light of His sovereignty, we take on a human viewpoint that severely limits, if not ignores, God's active involvement in our lives. The prophet Isaiah recounts a time when the nation of Israel did exactly this. The Hebrew people had come to the conclusion that God had forgotten and forsaken them (Isa. 49:14). In response to Israel's sense of alienation and despair, the Lord said,

"Can a woman forget her nursing child,
And have no compassion on the son of her womb?
Even these may forget, but I will not forget you.
Behold, I have inscribed you on the palms of My hands;
Your walls are continually before Me." (vv. 15–16)

We have come to the point in Solomon's journal where he once again acknowledges that God has everything under control (Eccles. 5:18–20, 6:10, 7:13–14). This recollection helps Solomon shift his perspective from the horizontal to the vertical. As the change occurs, divine wisdom starts recapturing the forefront in Solomon's life. We saw this evidenced in the first half of Ecclesiastes 7, where he gives a number of insightful proverbs on handling life. In the remainder of chapter 7, we will see Solomon's viewpoint come even more clearly into focus as he shows us how to put wisdom to work in everyday life. That's something we all can benefit from.

I. An Analysis of Wisdom

Since Solomon spends so much time in the latter half of his journal writing about wisdom, it would be a good idea for us to come to a basic understanding of its nature. If we were to peruse the pages of Scripture, we would find that *wisdom* is *"the God-given ability to see life with rare objectivity and to handle life with rare stability."* Godly discernment casts out fear and ushers in confidence. Whether we dip into a valley of deep poverty or soar to the pinnacle of great prosperity, we can find the perspective and steadiness we need to cope with life by drawing on God's wisdom.

II. The Outworking of Wisdom

How does godly wisdom work itself out in human life? Solomon addresses this question in Ecclesiastes 7:15–29. He shows us some characteristics that are produced by divine discernment. In doing so, he exposes several areas of our lives where wisdom can perform its perfecting work if we will cooperate by applying it. Let's probe into what Solomon says.

A. The balance wisdom gives. From a standpoint of uncompromising realism, the Preacher states, "I have seen everything during my lifetime of futility; there is a righteous man who

70

perishes in his righteousness, and there is a wicked man who prolongs his life in his wickedness" (v. 15). Virtually all of us have seen innocent people being treated unfairly and guilty people going unpunished. This sight usually dismays and angers us. It can also prompt us to become either overzealous in practicing righteousness or overindulgent in committing wickedness. With these potential responses in mind, Solomon exhorts us to live a life of balance: "Do not be excessively righteous, and do not be overly wise. Why should you ruin [or appall] yourself? Do not be excessively wicked, and do not be a fool. Why should you die before your time?" (vv. 16–17). Solomon is *not* advising us to obey God half-heartedly or sin against Him periodically. Rather, he is urging us to live our lives in light of God's omniscient and impartial judgment (cf. 11:9, 12:13–14). The Lord does not approve of a superspiritual lifestyle—one that is oriented toward impressing others with piety (cf. Matt. 5:20, Luke 18:9–14). Overly pious living can lead to frustration when one sees the righteous trampled underfoot. But neither does He sanction a lukewarm attitude toward sin (cf. 1 Cor. 5:1–8). For excessively foolish behavior can bring one's life to an end before its time (cf. Ps. 55:23, Prov. 10:27). Instead, God's desire is that we walk with Him in obedience and behave toward others with humility. When we fear the Lord in this way, we will achieve balance in our lives (Eccles. 7:18).

B. The strength wisdom produces. Continuing on in Ecclesiastes 7, we discover three areas of life that divine wisdom gives us the ability to handle. Indeed, one who operates from the sphere of godly discernment has more strength "than ten rulers who are in a city" (v. 19). Now that's power!

1. **Strength to handle the painful tensions.** Solomon speaks the truth when he writes, "There is not a righteous man on earth who continually does good and who never sins" (v. 20). Perfectionists have a hard time dealing with this reality. But the fact is that this is a tension we must live with. None of us have life "wired"; we all stumble and fall from time to time, and we always will until we die or are raptured. And yet, God calls on us to be perfect in all our behavior now (cf. Matt. 5:48, 1 Pet. 1:14–16). To help us come closer to this goal, God provides principles in the Bible that address the essentials of life (cf. 2 Tim. 3:16–17). But His guidelines require us to exercise wisdom in order to apply them accurately. And the more correctly we appropriate them, the more righteously we will live.

2. **Strength to avoid the pitfalls of gullibility.** To this wise counsel Solomon adds, "Do not take seriously all words

which are spoken" (Eccles. 7:21a). When we receive lavish praise, we should not let it inflate our egos nor ascribe to it undue importance. Wisdom equips us to keep our feet anchored in reality while others are trying to lift us into an undiscerning dreamworld.

3. **Strength to resist criticism.** This is Solomon's main point in verses 21–22. Observe what he says: "Do not take seriously all words which are spoken, lest you hear your servant cursing you. For you also have realized that you likewise have many times cursed others." Sometimes we receive unjustified and untimely criticism from others— even from those individuals who are closest to us. If we put stock in all the "bad press" we receive, we will end up with a distorted view of ourselves that could cause us to become intimidated, defeated, and guilt-ridden. Wisdom can help us separate valid and valuable criticism from that which is inaccurate and destructive. Solomon also reminds us in these verses that we are sometimes guilty of judging others falsely. Acknowledging this fact can prod us to abstain from giving false criticism as well as help us handle unjust remarks when we receive them.

C. **The insight wisdom offers.** In the remainder of Ecclesiastes 7, Solomon mentions three insights that divine wisdom can give us.

1. **We cannot understand ourselves, nor can we make ourselves wise.** This perception is embedded in these words: "I tested all this with wisdom, and I said, 'I will be wise,' but it was far from me. What has been is remote and exceedingly mysterious. Who can discover it?" (vv. 23–24). Solomon could not make himself wise, and neither can we produce godly discretion in our lives. Wisdom is a gift from God; no human being can manufacture it. Furthermore, we cannot fully understand ourselves. No amount of psychological analysis or introspection will ever unveil all that we are. To some degree, we will remain an enigma to ourselves until the One who knows us completely, fully reveals to us who we are (cf. 1 Cor. 13:12).

2. **Intimate relationships are compelling but often unsatisfying.** Solomon had a thousand women available to fulfill his every sexual desire and fantasy . . . to satisfy his every relational want and need. Did they bring him the contentment he sought? His answer is found in these remarks:

I directed my mind to know, to investigate, and
to seek wisdom and an explanation, and to know

the evil of folly and the foolishness of madness. And I discovered more bitter than death the woman whose heart is snares and nets, whose hands are chains. One who is pleasing to God will escape from her, but the sinner will be captured by her. (Eccles. 7:25–26)

Premarital escapades and extramarital affairs will not fulfill their promise to bring lasting satisfaction. Instead, they will both drag us away from a vital walk with God and bring confusion and hurt into the human relationships we hold most dear. Moreover, Solomon says that in his search for satisfaction in life, he did find " 'one man among a thousand' " who could help answer his questions (vv. 27–28a). But he did not come across even one woman in a thousand who could provide fulfillment (v. 28b). Perhaps the reason this occurred was because his preoccupation with sexual intimacy robbed him of the opportunity to experience the deep joys of marriage with one mate.

3. **Our basic problems are not outside of us but within us.** Wisdom provides us with the ability to see " 'that God made men upright, but they have sought out many devices' " (v. 29). God created man with the freedom to love and serve Him forever. But man turned his freedom against God and, as a result, has become creatively deceptive and destructive (cf. Gen. 1–4, Rom. 1:18–32). We cannot—indeed, dare not—blame the Lord for our sin. We are directly responsible for our own wrongdoing (cf. James 1:13–17).

III. Wisdom—Three Questions of Application

As we have seen, wisdom is not merely a theoretical concept to be covered up by dust in academic volumes. The Lord gives us wisdom so that we can view life with objectivity and handle it with stability. The good news is that all who place their trust in Jesus Christ as their Savior can lay claim to God's wisdom (1 Cor. 1:30). However, before divine wisdom will work itself out, this decision must be made by every individual. Those of us who have already placed our faith in Christ need to answer three questions concerning the outworking of wisdom in our everyday lives. If our responses are negative, then we need to ask ourselves why.

A. **Regarding balance: Is wisdom guarding me from extremes?**

B. **Regarding strength: Is wisdom keeping me stable?**

C. **Regarding insight: Is wisdom clearing my mind to see reality?**

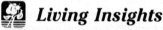

Living Insights

Study One

We defined *wisdom* as "the God-given ability to see life with rare objectivity and to handle life with rare stability." An excellent scriptural example of this is found in the entire second chapter of 1 Corinthians. Let's turn to that storehouse of information on wisdom.

- Copy the chart below into your notebook. As you read through the sixteen verses of 1 Corinthians 2, jot down the thoughts that best describe both human wisdom and godly wisdom.

| 1 Corinthians 2 ||
Human Wisdom	Godly Wisdom

Living Insights

Study Two

When God started things off, everything was right-side up. But somehow in the process, man attempted to fill his life with other "devices" and turned it all upside down! Instead of putting our lives in *His* hands, we want to keep them in *our* hands. However, we can overcome this tendency through the application of godly wisdom. In light of this fact, take a few moments to answer these simple questions. The answers may be troubling at first, but the overall result can be a positive experience.

- Is wisdom guarding you from extremes? How?
- Is wisdom keeping you stable? How?
- Is wisdom clearing your mind to see reality? How?

The Qualities of a Good Boss
Ecclesiastes 8:1–9

All too frequently, bosses fall into one of two categories. Some are simply *incompetent*. They are not qualified for the tasks they are supposed to perform. Such superiors are difficult to work for, because they are usually negative and discouraging rather than positive and encouraging. Many other bosses are *intolerant*. They are generally knowledgeable of their position and competent to perform their required tasks but are nearly impossible to please. Because they are so high-achieving, hard-charging, and tough-minded, they usually demand more from others than can reasonably be expected. But lest we come down too hard on these types of leaders, we must admit that becoming a good boss is neither accidental nor automatic. It takes a great deal of time, patience, and work. What makes a leader someone people want to follow? What are the qualities of a good boss? King Solomon deals with this matter in the eighth chapter of his journal. What he says applies to all of us who are now in positions of authority or who expect to be in the future. So let's pay attention to Solomon's words. If we apply them consistently, we will become better models of godly leadership at home, on the job, or in some form of Christian ministry.

I. Characteristics of a Wise Leader

Involved in Solomon's shift in perspective is a logical change of focus from human folly to divine wisdom. This radical alteration naturally leads the Israelite king to consider the traits of a wise leader. We know that he is dealing with people in leadership positions because of some of the phrases he uses: " 'the command of the king' " (Eccles. 8:2a), "the word of the king is authoritative" (v. 4a), "he who keeps a royal command" (v. 5a), and "a man has exercised authority over another man" (v. 9b). As Solomon speaks to the issue of sound leadership, he mentions at least five characteristics of a qualified, godly superior.

A. A clear mind. The quality of mental clarity can be found in these words: "Who is like the wise man and who knows the interpretation of a matter?" (v. 1a). The key to this question is wrapped up in the word *interpretation*. The Hebrew word for this term comes from *pah-shaar*, an Aramaic word that means "solution." It is often used to refer to someone who sees through the mystery of something and is able to explain it (cf. Dan. 5:12). In this context, the word denotes an individual who knows why a thing is the way it is. When this idea is applied to leaders, it means that good superiors know philosophically where they are leading those under them and why. They do not need to have an exhaustive understanding of all the *how-tos*, but they do

75

need to know the answers to the *whys.* This requires that those in charge take the time necessary to think about leadership, staffing, goals, purpose, and anything else that is pertinent to their responsibilities. After all, clarity at the top is needed if there is to be definition of purpose and responsibility at the bottom. On the other hand, if there is confusion among those in authority, one can be certain that there is even greater perplexity among those under their direction.

B. A cheerful disposition. Solomon adds that "a man's wisdom illumines him [literally, his face] and causes his stern face to beam" (Eccles. 8:1b). The root of the Hebrew word for *stern* is translated "fierce countenance" and "insolent" in other portions of Scripture (Deut. 28:50a, Dan. 8:23b). Consequently, we can appropriately paraphrase Solomon's words this way: "A man's wisdom lights up his face and causes his otherwise fierce countenance to radiate." Fewer things are more contagious than cheerfulness. When leaders are happy, they generally have a positive impact on their followers. Similarly, tough, frowning bosses can promote a negative atmosphere and a spirit of intimidation among their employees. The Lord desires that His people take Him seriously but that they not take themselves too seriously. He wants them to wipe off their grim looks, put smiles on their faces, and let laughter flow from their lips. In light of this counsel, many of us would do well to ponder these comments from the pen of Helmut Thielicke:

> Should we not see that lines of laughter about the
> eyes are just as much marks of faith as are the lines
> of care and seriousness? Is it only earnestness that
> is baptized? Is laughter pagan? We have already
> allowed too much that is good to be lost to the
> church and cast many pearls before swine. A church
> is in a bad way when it banishes laughter from the
> sanctuary and leaves it to the cabaret, the nightclub
> and the toastmasters.[1]

If our faces are tight and stern, we are probably not acting with wisdom. A wise person—especially a discerning superior—has a pleasurable temperament.

C. A discreet mouth. The next piece of counsel we find speaks directly to subordinates, but it also has an indirect application to superiors. Consider what Solomon writes:

> I say, "Keep the command of the king because of the
> oath before God. Do not be in a hurry to leave him.
> Do not join in an evil matter, for he will do whatever

1. Helmut Thielicke, *Encounter with Spurgeon* (Philadelphia: Fortress Press, 1963), p. 26.

he pleases." Since the word of the king is authoritative, who will say to him, "What are you doing?" (Eccles. 8:2–4)

The advice to followers is clear: Obey your leaders and remain loyal to them. Why? If for no other reason than that they have the ability to make life difficult for you. Aside from this obvious instruction is a latent application: The speech of superiors has a direct effect on the loyalty and cooperation they receive from their subordinates. In other words, employees respect a boss with a discreet mouth. Leaders who exercise their authority with tact, sensitivity, and compassion will generally receive the benefit of supportive followers.

D. Keen judgment. The quality of keen judgment is conveyed in these verses: "He who keeps a royal command experiences no trouble, for a wise heart knows the proper time and procedure. For there is a proper time and procedure for every delight, when a man's trouble is heavy upon him. If no one knows what will happen, who can tell him when it will happen?" (vv. 5–7). As we review these comments, we discover four facts about quality leaders. First, leaders have a "royal command" (v. 5a). Their positions of authority are God-given (cf. Ps. 75:6–7), and as such, their leadership should be marked by godly discernment. Second, effective leaders know "the proper time and procedure" for accomplishing what needs to be done (Eccles. 8:5b–6a). Third, wise superiors remain stable under pressure (v. 6). Difficult situations do not panic them; instead, they continue to think clearly and make tough decisions with a calm, steady resolve. Fourth, insightful leaders have independent intuition (v. 7). They are so sensitive and tuned-in that they can simply sense the attitude of their followers.

E. A humble spirit. Notice how Solomon refers to the quality of humility: "No man has authority to restrain the wind with the wind, or authority over the day of death; and there is no discharge in the time of war, and evil will not deliver those who practice it" (v. 8). In other words, all of us have limitations. Regardless of how gifted, skillful, and influential we are, none of us can do whatever we want whenever we would like to do it. Good leaders never forget this fact, and it is reflected in their humble, teachable spirits. Such superiors draw on the strengths of their subordinates and, in so doing, give them a genuine sense of dignity and importance. Moreover, wise leaders depend on the Lord to guide them through the responsibilities and rigors of their positions. They realize that their authority is ultimately derived from Him and that they can do absolutely nothing without Him (Matt. 28:18, John 15:5).

77

*very special for leaders   Evil won't deliver you

II. Two Warnings for Those in Authority

In Ecclesiastes 8:8b–9, Solomon's comments suggest two warnings to all who are leaders. First, *it is inexcusable for leaders to take unfair advantage of those under their charge* (v. 8b). Superiors may try to abuse and oppress their workers. They might even rewrite the rules, calling good evil, and evil good. But their conduct and rationalizations will not be sanctioned or excused by God. Second, *leaders who take unfair advantage of their followers hurt themselves more than they hurt those under their authority* (v. 9). People who initiate unjust policies and practices will not get away with it. The Lord promises that they will be punished in this life, the next one, or both (12:14; Amos 5:10–15, 18–20, 8:4–14; Matt. 12:36–37; 2 Cor. 5:10).   VALUE of Being a MODEL (not getting a job done)

III. Personal Appropriation of These Qualities

It's a tough assignment both to be in a position of authority and, at the same time, to be competent and fair. But most of us have been called to be exactly that—whether it is at home, in the office, at church, or anywhere else. So as we meditate on how to apply the characteristics of a good leader in our lives, let's ponder two final, all-important thoughts.

A. We must never forget the value of being a role model. High-achieving, hard-charging leaders frequently over-emphasize the finished product while abusing the people they have instructed to complete the project. Admittedly, tasks need to get done. But effective leaders realize that the accomplishment of a job is less important than the model they provide for those under their charge. The influence we have on the lives of others will outlive their memory of our achievements. We need to work hard at being examples worth modeling and stop striving to meet objectives at the expense of other people.

B. We must never lose the vision of seeing a cycle. One day, our leadership roles will be taken over by other individuals. In fact, good superiors seek to work themselves out of a leadership position by training others to take over. In a church, this cyclical process is called discipleship. When it happens in a home, it's referred to as rearing a family. Regardless of the label it is given, the cultivation of new leaders is a significant task. By modeling wise leadership and teaching others how to become godly leaders, we influence the future more than we will ever know. Will you accept the challenge to be a good boss? And, if you are an employee, will you apply yourself to becoming a faithful and diligent worker? Both jobs are demanding, but the rewards are great.

Vision of seeing a cycle in your leadership –

The Model is essential

Our example outlives our accomplishments

78

You have to get the job done —
That's your profession.) — making Christ
KNOWN

 Living Insights   *Do not model materialism,*
but Model Care + Compassion
Depth —

Study One ▬▬▬▬▬▬▬

Our primary focus in this study has been on the qualities of a good employer. But there's another aspect worth considering in this passage—the qualities of a good *employee.*

- After you copy the following chart into your notebook, read through Ecclesiastes 8:1–9 and look for characteristics of a good subordinate. You may be surprised to find how much of Solomon's counsel applies to employees.

Qualities of a Good Employee	
Qualities	Verses

Living Insights

Study Two ▬▬▬▬▬▬▬

Our example outlives our achievements. Pause and let that statement sink in. As moms, dads, grandparents, teachers, pastors, chief executive officers, coaches, and bosses, we are models that others are watching.

- Stop and think: Who were/are your models? Jot down their names and the most admirable qualities they passed on to you.

Names	Qualities

Continued on next page

- Now, who are the people looking up to you as a model? Write down their names and the most admirable qualities you are attempting to pass on to them.

Names	Qualities

Mysteries That Defy Explanation
Ecclesiastes 8:10–17

"Oh, the depth of the riches both of the wisdom and knowledge of God! How unsearchable are His judgments and unfathomable His ways!" (Rom. 11:33). So exclaims the Apostle Paul. Although well educated, widely traveled, and extremely wise, he did not hesitate to acknowledge and exalt the incomprehensible nature and activity of God. In the eighth chapter of Ecclesiastes, Solomon comes to a similar understanding after considering some enigmas involving both a world marred by sin and the Lord who rules over it. The observations he makes and the counsel he renders form a realistic, relevant basis for dealing with mysteries.

I. Some Thoughts about Mysteries

Spirit of God does it ⅄ it is the Spirit of God revealing to you

Before we dig into Solomon's diary, let's gain some insight into the different kinds of mysteries that exist. By doing so, we will come to a better understanding of Solomon's comments and their application to our lives.

A. A few important distinctions. Anything that deserves the label "mysterious" is at least temporarily baffling. Murder-mystery novels display this quality, for they present a perplexing crime that eventually winds up being solved. This kind of mystery is usually resolvable through human means of investigation and deduction. There are other mysteries, however, that cannot be explained by human reason or experience alone. It is not that man is incapable of knowing them, but that he cannot understand them without God's aid. In biblical times, this divine help frequently came in the form of revelation that gave man the knowledge he needed to at least partially comprehend God's message and activity (cf. Dan. 2:4–47, Matt. 13:10–23, Rom. 16:25–26, 1 Cor. 15:51–54, Eph. 3:3–12, Col. 2:2–3, 1 Tim. 3:16, Rev. 1:20). There are still other mysteries that are absolutely beyond man's ability to fully understand. For example, because man is finite, he will never be capable of completely knowing the nature and ways of the infinite God (cf. Job 11:7–11, Isa. 55:8–9, Rom. 11:33–36).[1]

. For more information on the concept of mystery in the Bible, see the essay titled "Secret, Mystery," by Günter Finkenrath, in *The New International Dictionary of New Testament Theology,* edited by Colin Brown, 3 vols. (Grand Rapids: Zondervan Publishing House, 1978), vol. 3, pp. 501–6. Some people suggest that the mysterious elements of Christianity were borrowed from the pagan mystery religions of the ancient Greek world. Three books that refute this position are the following: *The Origin of Paul's Religion,* by J. Gresham Machen (New York: Macmillan Publishing Co., 1925); *Pre-Christian Gnosticism: A Survey of the Proposed Evidences,* by Edwin M. Yamauchi, 2d ed. (Grand Rapids: Baker Book House, 1983); and *Christianity and the Hellenistic World,* by Ronald H. Nash, Christian Free University Curriculum (Grand Rapids: Zondervan Publishing House; Dallas: Probe Ministries International, 1984).

*Man cannot explain
God's Mysteries*

B. An essential clarification. Contrary to what some people believe, the Bible never indicates that divine mysteries are paradoxical or contradictory. The Lord may reveal certain truths that go *beyond* our ability to fully comprehend, but He never unveils anything that goes *against* sound reason. Indeed, God exhorted young Timothy, through the Apostle Paul, to avoid "opposing arguments"—literally, antitheses or contradictions (1 Tim. 6:20). And John, the beloved disciple of Christ, wrote that the Son of God is the eternal "Word"—that is, the Logic Reason, or Rational Discourse of God (John 1:1).[2] In other words the invisible Creator is intrinsically rational, and thus, His divine Son is the visible manifestation of His perfect rationality (v. 14) And since the Lord is unchanging and faithful, He will not—indeed, cannot—violate His logically consistent nature by thinking, speaking, or acting in contradictory ways (cf. 2 Tim. 2:13, Titus 1:2, Heb. 6:16–18).

II. Solomon's Additional Mysteries

With this crucial information in mind, we are almost ready to examine the mysteries that Solomon puts before us in Ecclesiastes 8. However, we will get a firmer grip on these enigmas if we approach them from the proper viewpoint. Solomon gives us this perspective in his closing remarks. Notice what he writes:

> When I gave my heart to know wisdom and to see the task which has been done on the earth (even though one should never sleep day or night), and I saw every work of God, I concluded that man cannot discover the work which has been done under the sun. Even though man should seek laboriously, he will not discover; and though the wise man should say, "I know," he cannot discover. (Eccles. 8:16–17)

The outlook we should have on divine mysteries is twofold. First we should understand that *God's mysteries defy human explanation.* No matter how hard we try or how long we labor, we cannot figure out the infinite workings of God. With His help, we can understand His activity in part, but a full grasp of it is beyond our ability. This point leads to the second matter we must realize—namely, that *God's mysteries go beyond human intellect and wisdom.* We cannot discover them on our own. If He wants us to know them at all, then

2. The Greek term in John 1:1 for "Word" is *Lógos.* Some helpful discussions on its meaning and interpretation can be found in these sources: "Lógos," by Bertold Klappert and Colin Brown, in *The New International Dictionary of New Testament Theology,* vol. 3, pp. 1081–1119 *New Testament Theology,* by Donald Gutherie (Downers Grove: InterVarsity Press, 1981 pp. 321–29; *The Philosophy of Gordon H. Clark: A Festschrift,* edited by Ronald H. Nash (Philadelphia: The Presbyterian and Reformed Publishing Co., 1968), p. 67.

He must reveal them to us. Of course, the mysteries we cannot resolve frequently cause us to struggle in our faith. Solomon mentions three that are likely to trouble us.

A. **The mystery of unjust triumph.** Solomon first describes an all-too-familiar scene: "So then, I have seen the wicked buried, those who used to go in and out from the holy place, and they are soon forgotten in the city where they did thus. This too is futility [or mysterious]" (v. 10). Evil people often attend religious institutions and functions in order to cover up their wickedness and bring a degree of respectability to their lives. Then when they die and are buried, they frequently receive such an impressive funeral that the sins they committed are quickly forgotten, even in the places which were most affected by their wrongdoing. To make matters worse, those who are unjust often escape punishment and live long, prosperous lives (vv. 11a, 12a). This frequently leads individuals to intensify and multiply their wrongdoing (v. 11b). When we consider these observations in light of God's hatred of sin and His promise to punish evildoers (cf. Exod. 34:7, Deut. 28:15–68, Prov. 11:20–21), we find it baffling—even unfair—that the Lord does not swiftly judge them (cf. Hab. 1).

B. **The mystery of unfair consequences.** Solomon observes another occurrence that provokes our puzzlement and anger: "There is futility which is done on the earth, that is, there are righteous men to whom it happens according to the deeds of the wicked. On the other hand, there are evil men to whom it happens according to the deeds of the righteous. I say that this too is futility [or mysterious]" (Eccles. 8:14). Why are godly missionaries martyred while brutal murderers live on unpunished? Why is it that an irresponsible drunk driver walks away from an accident without a scratch, while the Christian family he hit dies in the collision? Why must a hard-working, honest woman barely scrape enough money together to meet her children's needs, while vicious, dishonest gangsters are able to live in luxury from the money brought in by gambling, prostitution, and drugs? For those of us who believe in an all-good, sovereign God, these questions raise issues that we are unable to fully resolve.

C. **The mystery of untimely pleasure.** Solomon's response to the other two mysteries is a mystery in itself. He communicates it this way: "So I commended pleasure, for there is nothing good for a man under the sun except to eat and to drink and to be merry, and this will stand by him in his toils throughout the days of his life which God has given him under the sun" (v. 15). Solomon is not exhorting us to embrace a hedonistic lifestyle. Rather, he is advising us to enjoy life and to trust in God even in the face of unsolvable mysteries. But why should we follow his counsel? Because if we don't, we could become resentful, pessimistic, and increasingly wicked in reaction to unjust triumphs and unfair consequences. Obviously, this response would not benefit us at all. On the other hand, there are temporal and everlasting advantages "for those who fear God . . . openly" (v. 12b) in spite of their unanswered questions. Therefore, we should be content with the basics of life and receive them as gifts from God's hand (cf. 3:12–13, 5:18–20).

III. Ways to Handle Life's Mysteries

We can add three final suggestions that will serve to round out Solomon's counsel on dealing with the troubling enigmas of life

A. We must admit that we are only human.

B. We must admit that we don't understand why, and we may never learn why while on this earth.

C. We must admit that there are some things we cannot change no matter how hard we try.

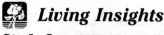 *Living Insights*

Study One ▬▬▬▬▬▬▬▬▬▬▬▬▬▬▬▬▬▬▬▬▬▬▬▬▬▬▬▬▬

Mystery. Have you ever examined the use of the term in God's Word? It appears several times in a variety of contexts. Let's use the term *mystery* as a stepping stone for a scriptural search.

• Consult a Bible concordance for the references to *mystery* and *mysteries.* Make a copy of the following chart and enter the references in the left column. In the center column, write what is being described as a mystery. Finally, use the right column to enter your personal thoughts on the mysteries you find.

Mysteries in the Bible		
References	Mysteries	Observations

Living Insights

This study has allowed us to observe Solomon as he learns to deal with mysteries that defy explanation. Let's test our ability to handle life's enigmas. Take a few moments to ask yourself the following questions:

- What mysteries have you encountered that defy human understanding?
- Have you experienced or observed the mystery of unjust triumph?
- Have you been confronted with the mystery of unfair consequences?
- Have you dealt with the mystery of untimely pleasure?
- In all of the above issues, how have you guarded yourself against wrong responses?
- What are some valuable lessons you have learned through all of these circumstances?

Digging Deeper

Our study in this portion of Solomon's journal raises a number of crucial questions concerning revelation, reason, and faith. For example: What is reason? What is faith? Are reason and faith complementary, or do they logically oppose each other? Did the laws of logic originate in God's nature or in man's mind? Does divine truth contradict, complement, and/or comply with human reason? How has sin affected man's ability to think correctly and clearly? Can human beings understand anything about God before placing their faith in Him? Should Christians reason about their faith and seek to defend it rationally? Should skeptics have good reasons to believe in Christianity before they trust in Christ as their Savior? Throughout much of Church history, Christian theologians, philosophers, apologists, and ministers have generally agreed that sound reason confirms and complements divine revelation and faith. However, many Christians today have departed from this traditional stand for a variety of reasons. To help you come to some conclusions on this practical matter, we have provided two lists—one that gives some important Bible passages, and another that names several valuable resources. We would encourage you to conduct a personal or group study of the scriptural texts first. Your familiarity with these passages will help you better evaluate the diverse positions that are represented in the extra-biblical materials. We should warn you that this issue can become quite complex. But if you would like to dig further, you can unearth some gems that will strengthen your faith and enhance your witness.

- **Pertinent Passages**
  Psalm 19:1–6; Isaiah 1:18; Matthew 22:29, 35–38; Luke 1:1–4;
  John 1:1, 3:14–18, 20:24–31; Acts 1:3, 7, 6:13–7:53, 14:14–17, 17:1–4,
  10–12, 16–34, 18:4, 13, 19, 27–28, 19:8–10, 25–27, 22:1–21, 26:1–29,
  28:23–24; Romans 1:18–32, 12:1–2; 1 Corinthians 1:17–31, 2:1–16,
  15:3–19; 2 Corinthians 4:3–4, 10:5; Galatians 3:1–26; Ephe-
  sians 4:17–24; Colossians 2:8; 2 Thessalonians 2:13; 1 Timothy 6:20;
  2 Timothy 2:13; Titus 1:9; Hebrews 11:1–40; James 2:14–26;
  1 John 1:1–4
- **Relevant Resources**
  Ayers, Robert H. "Language, Logic and Reason in Calvin's *Institutes.*"
  Religious Studies 16 (September 1980), pp. 283–97.
  Barclay, Oliver R. *The Intellect and Beyond.* Grand Rapids: Academie
  Books, Zondervan Publishing House, 1985.
  Bavinck, Herman. *The Doctrine of God.* Translated by William
  Hendriksen. Grand Rapids: Baker Book House, 1979. Pp. 13–80.
  Bush, L. Russ, ed. *Classical Readings in Christian Apologetics, A.D.
  100–1800.* Grand Rapids: Academie Books, Zondervan Publishing
  House, 1983.
  Calvin, John. *Calvin: Institutes of the Christian Religion.* 2 vols. Edited
  by John T. McNeill. Translated by Ford Lewis Battles. The Library
  of Christian Classics. Philadelphia: The Westminster Press, 1960.
  Vol. 1, pp. 33–802.
  Corduan, Winfried. *Handmaid to Theology: An Essay in Philosophical
  Prolegomena.* Foreword by Norman L. Geisler. Grand Rapids:
  Baker Book House, 1981.
  Dahms, John F. "How Reliable is Logic?" *Journal of the Evangelical
  Theological Society* 21 (December 1978), pp. 369–80.
  Dahms, John F. "A Trinitarian Epistemology Defended: A Rejoinder
  to Norman Geisler." *Journal of the Evangelical Theological Society*
  22 (June 1979), pp. 133–48.
  Davis, John Jefferson. *Foundations of Evangelical Theology.* Grand
  Rapids: Baker Book House, 1984.
  Demarest, Bruce A. *General Revelation: Historical Views and
  Contemporary Issues.* Foreword by Vernon C. Grounds. Grand
  Rapids: Zondervan Publishing House, 1982.
  Garrigou-Lagrange, R. *God: His Existence and His Nature.* 2 vols.
  Translated by Dom Bede Rose. St. Louis: B. Herder Book Co., 1948.
  Vol 1.
  Geehan, E. R., ed. *Jerusalem and Athens: Critical Discussions on the
  Philosophy and Apologetics of Cornelius Van Til.* Nutley:
  Presbyterian and Reformed Publishing Co., 1977.
  Geisler, Norman L. "Avoid *All* Contradictions: A Surrejoinder to John
  Dahms." *Journal of the Evangelical Theological Society* 22 (June
  1979), pp. 149–59.

Geisler, Norman L. " 'Avoid . . . Contradictions' (1 Timothy 6:20): A Reply to John Dahms." *Journal of the Evangelical Theological Society* 22 (March 1979), pp. 55–65.

Geisler, Norman L. *Christian Apologetics.* Grand Rapids: Baker Book House, 1976.

Geisler, Norman L., ed. *What Augustine Says.* Grand Rapids: Baker Book House, 1982. Chap. 1.

Geisler, Norman L., and Feinberg, Paul D. *Introduction to Philosophy: A Christian Perspective.* Grand Rapids: Baker Book House, 1980. Chaps. 1–10, 16–17, 19.

Gerrish, Brian A. *Grace and Reason: A Study in the Theology of Luther.* Midway Reprint. Chicago: The University of Chicago Press, 1979.

Gilson, Étienne. *God and Philosophy.* New Haven: Yale University Press, 1941.

Grounds, Vernon C. "The Postulate of Paradox." *Bulletin of the Evangelical Theological Society* 7 (Winter 1964), pp. 3–21.

Hanna, Mark M. *Crucial Questions in Apologetics.* Grand Rapids: Baker Book House, 1981.

Hodge, Charles. *Systematic Theology.* 3 vols. Reprint. Grand Rapids: William B. Eerdmans Publishing Co., 1979. Pp. 1–365.

Hoover, A. J. *Don't You Believe It!* Chicago: Moody Press, 1982.

Howe, Frederic R. *Challenge and Response: A Handbook of Christian Apologetics.* Grand Rapids: Zondervan Publishing House, 1982.

Katz, Steven T. "The Language and Logic of 'Mystery' in Christology." In *Christ, Faith and History.* Edited by S. W. Sykes and J. P. Clayton. Cambridge Studies in Christology. Cambridge: Cambridge University Press, 1972. Pp. 239–61.

Lewis, C. S. *Mere Christianity.* New York: Macmillan Publishing Co., 1952.

Lewis, Gordon R. *Testing Christianity's Truth Claims: Approaches to Christian Apologetics.* Chicago: Moody Press, 1976.

Machen, J. Gresham. *What is Faith?* Grand Rapids: William B. Eerdmans Publishing Co., 1925.

Mayers, Ronald B. *Both/And: A Balanced Apologetic.* Foreword by Kenneth Kantzer. Chicago: Moody Press, 1984.

Morris, Thomas V. *Francis Schaeffer's Apologetics: A Critique.* Chicago: Moody Press, 1976.

Montgomery, John Warwick. *Faith Founded on Fact: Essays in Evidential Apologetics.* Nashville: Thomas Nelson, Inc., 1978.

Nash, Ronald H., ed. *The Philosophy of Gordon H. Clark: A Festschrift.* Philadelphia: The Presbyterian and Reformed Publishing Co., 1968.

Purtill, Richard L. *C. S. Lewis's Case for the Christian Faith.* San Francisco: Harper and Row, 1981.

Ramm, Bernard. *Varieties of Christian Apologetics.* Grand Rapids: Baker Book House, 1962.

Reymond, Robert L. *The Justification of Knowledge.* Philadelphia: The Presbyterian and Reformed Publishing Co., 1976.

Schaeffer, Francis A. *Escape from Reason.* Downers Grove: InterVarsity Press, 1968.

Schaeffer, Francis A. *The God Who Is There.* Downers Grove: InterVarsity Press, 1968.

Shedd, William G. T. *Dogmatic Theology.* 3 vols. Classic Reprint Edition. Minneapolis: Klock and Klock Christian Publishers, 1979. Vol. 1.

Sproul, R. C.; Gerstner, John; and Lindsley, Arthur. *Classical Apologetics: A Rational Defense of the Christian Faith and a Critique of Presuppositional Apologetics.* Grand Rapids: Academie Books, Zondervan Publishing House, 1984.

Stott, John R. W. *Your Mind Matters.* Downers Grove: InterVarsity Press, 1972.

Thomas Aquinas. *Aquinas on Nature and Grace.* Edited by A. M. Fairweather. The Library of Christian Classics: Ichthus Edition. Philadelphia: The Westminster Press, 1954.

Vos, Arvin. *Aquinas, Calvin, and Contemporary Protestant Thought: A Critique of Protestant Views on the Thought of Thomas Aquinas.* Foreword by Ralph McInery. Washington: Christian University Press, a subsidiary of the Christian College Consortium and William B. Eerdmans Publishing Co., 1985.

Warfield, Benjamin Breckinridge. *Calvin and Augustine.* Edited by Samuel G. Craig. Foreword by J. Marcellus Kik. Philadelphia: The Presbyterian and Reformed Publishing Co., 1956.

Have a Blast While You Last!

Ecclesiastes 9:1–10

In construction work, it is often necessary to do some blasting before rebuilding can begin. New and beautiful structures cannot be erected where old and ugly ones still stand. This truth also applies to our outlook on life. Frequently, we need to destroy "speculations and every lofty thing raised up against the knowledge of God" before taking our "every thought captive to the obedience of Christ" (2 Cor. 10:5). Solomon discovered the value of this process in his search for lasting satisfaction. But rather than working through the human approaches to life philosophically, he did so experientially. Solomon's findings are recorded in his journal, Ecclesiastes. Here he blasts away at several under-the-sun lifestyles, concluding that they are all exercises in futility. So what's left? If man does not have a way to achieve satisfaction in life, then who does? And how should man conduct himself this side of death? Not surprisingly, Solomon addresses these questions. However, the advice he gives might shock many of us. So hold on to your seats as we continue our journey through this ancient diary.

I. Familiar Philosophies of Life That Do Not Work

Let's recall four under-the-sun pursuits that left Solomon feeling empty and frustrated. Each of these approaches is still popular, indicating once again that "there is nothing new under the sun" (Eccles. 1:9b). And each of these philosophies needs to be eradicated from our lives before we can build a life of meaning and contentment.

A. Materialism. This philosophy says, "Possessions satisfy—supply yourself!" Those who embrace this view are on a perpetual binge of accumulating things. To them, relationships with other people are important only insofar as they make it possible to gain material goods. In other words, people are used and things are loved. This is just the opposite of God's value system, which He has always intended for man to adopt (see Gen. 1:26–30; Amos 5:10–15, 6:4–7, 8:4–10; Matt. 6:24–33).

B. Hedonism. Many people refer to this outlook as the playboy philosophy. It says simply, "Life is a ball—enjoy yourself!" This perspective encourages us to throw moral restraint to the wind and unleash our freedom in whatever ways we desire. Ironically, those who exercise this type of "liberty" become enslaved to their passions. They also use people to satisfy their wants rather than treating them as ends which are valuable in themselves.

C. Humanism. This perspective says, "Humanity is glorious—exalt yourself!" The humanistic philosopher Corliss Lamont clearly expresses the central belief of this understanding: "Humanism, having its ultimate faith in man, believes that human beings possess the power or potentiality of solving their own problems." Man can accomplish this goal "through reliance primarily upon reason and scientific method applied with courage and vision."[1] Humanists believe that people are the masters of their own fate. They can deliver themselves from their struggles by thinking and working together. One problem, however, is that man has repeatedly failed to find lasting solutions apart from God. Indeed, his alleged solutions have often led to his own devaluation rather than exaltation.[2]

D. Fatalism. Like the other philosophies we have mentioned, this one has had proponents for centuries. It says, "The game is fixed—resign yourself!" Fatalists generally believe that events are determined by uncaring deities or irrational forces of nature. Their position leaves no room for human freedom or responsibility. What will be, will be—regardless. Therefore, people should just accept whatever comes, be it happiness or misery, wealth or poverty. Because fatalism drains hope and motivation from people's lives, it has led many to despair and even suicide.

II. An Alternate Philosophy on Living That Does Work

Materialism, hedonism, humanism, and fatalism—Solomon has blasted these philosophies and many others in his journal. Now it is time for him to rebuild. The Israelite ruler began some construction on the foundations of divine wisdom in Ecclesiastes 7–8. But in chapter 9, his turn from the ruins of horizontal outlooks to the sturdy foundation of the vertical viewpoint comes to a conclusion. We know this because of his opening words: "For I have taken all this to my heart and explain it" (9:1a). In effect Solomon is saying, "I have investigated these human approaches to life and found them all to be futile. Not one of them leads to lasting satisfaction. However, in my search, I discovered a path that does bring contentment. Let me save you some heartache by introducing you to a philosophy that works because it fits with reality." What is this philosophy? Let's find out. Solomon tells us that this biblical perspective on life has at least four major elements.

A. The sovereign hand of God. "Righteous men, wise men, and their deeds are in the hand of God. Man does not know whether it will be love or hatred; anything awaits him" (v. 1b). These statements do not mean that man is a helpless puppet

1. Corliss Lamont, *The Philosophy of Humanism* (New York: Philosophical Library, 1949), p. 12. Perhaps the finest contemporary critique of secular and Christian forms of humanism is given by Norman L. Geisler in his book *Is Man the Measure? An Evaluation of Contemporary Humanism* (Grand Rapids: Baker Book House, 1983).

2. Francis Schaeffer supports and illustrates this truth in his book *How Should We Then Live? The Rise and Decline of Western Thought and Culture* (Old Tappan: Fleming H. Revell Co., 1976).

who performs whatever the divine Puppeteer wants him to do. This caricature portrays both God and man inaccurately. For the Bible teaches that man is free and morally responsible for his actions (cf. Gen. 3, Matt. 23:37–39, Acts 7:51–53). Scripture also states that the Lord does not directly cause all events to occur—such as the evil deeds of man (cf. James 1:13–17). But God does intervene in history in order to accomplish His all-good, perfect will, and He does cause all things to work together for the benefit of those who have placed their faith in Him (cf. Gen. 45:4–11, 50:18–21; Rom. 8:28–30). Thus, Solomon's comments convey the truth that nothing happens to human beings which has not first been permitted by the Lord. And unless God reveals otherwise, man does not know beforehand what will occur in his life. It could be economic prosperity and physical health, or financial loss and terminal illness (see Job 1, Deut. 28). Whatever the case, it is comforting to know that the compassionate, righteous Lord is in control.

B. The absolute certainty of death.

> It is the same for all. There is one fate for the righteous and for the wicked; for the good, for the clean, and for the unclean; for the man who offers a sacrifice and for the one who does not sacrifice. As the good man is, so is the sinner; as the swearer is, so is the one who is afraid to swear. This is an evil in all that is done under the sun, that there is one fate for all men. (Eccles. 9:2–3a)

Since the first sin of Adam and Eve, death has become an inescapable fact of human life (Gen. 2:16–17, 3:1–19; Ps. 89:48; Rom. 5:12). It makes no difference whether we are righteous or wicked, saintly or sinful; death awaits each of us. Coming to grips with this fact can help us straighten out our priorities and live more wisely.

C. The evil and insanity of the human heart. Solomon does not mince words on this issue: "The hearts of the sons of men are full of evil, and insanity is in their hearts throughout their lives. Afterwards they go to the dead" (Eccles. 9:3b). This is what the doctrine of total depravity is all about. Man has turned his back on the living God—the One who knows him best and desires to give him the best. Rather than reap the abundant riches of the infinitely loving Lord, man has sought his own means of obtaining happiness and contentment. But like the prodigal son who foolishly squandered his share of his father's estate, man has lost his potential blessings by rebelling against the sovereign God. In order for reconciliation to take place, people must turn from their wicked madness and come to their senses as the prodigal son did (Luke 15:11–24). Until this step is taken, they have no hope of receiving a cure for their insanity.

D. Genuine hope for the living.

> Whoever is joined with [all] the living, there is hope; surely a live dog is better than a dead lion. For the living know they will die; but the dead do not know anything, nor have they any longer a reward, for their memory is forgotten. Indeed their love, their hate, and their zeal have already perished, and they will no longer have a share in all that is done under the sun. (Eccles. 9:4–6)

During Solomon's day, dogs were not treated as pets but were despised as mad and diseased mongrels. Lions, on the other hand, were regarded as animals of royalty and were thereby treated with respect. With this analogy, Solomon is saying that it is better to be dishonored and alive than honored and dead. Why? Because the living have hope. They have things that they can look forward to enjoying while on earth. But the dead have no such hope. Those who have passed on can no longer share in the joys of earthly pleasures. In fact, even their passions— love, hate, and zeal—are stilled by death. Our realization of this fact can prompt us to appreciate life in the present rather than postpone our enjoyment to a future time that may never come.

III. Great Counsel on How to Live 365 Days a Year

How should this biblical philosophy of life affect the way we live? The answer Solomon gives to this question may surprise many of us, but it is God's counsel on how to experience a wonderful life while living under the sun.

A. Live happily wherever you are. Notice the first part of Solomon's advice for living: "Go then, eat your bread in happiness, and drink your wine with a cheerful heart; for God has already approved your works" (Eccles. 9:7). This is definitely uncommon advice in conservative Christian circles. Nevertheless, God has approved it since He is the One who has given people the ability to enjoy the fruits of their labor (2:24–25, 3:12–13, 5:18–19). So the Lord is pleased when we find pleasure in His good gifts.

B. Walk in purity and in the power of the Spirit. Lest we conclude that Solomon is encouraging hedonism, we should note that he immediately adds these words of exhortation: "Let your clothes be white all the time, and let not oil be lacking on your head" (9:8). This verse is not to be interpreted literally. White clothes often symbolize moral purity and spiritual righteousness in Scripture (Isa. 1:18; Rev. 3:4–5, 7:9–14), and oil typologically represents the ministry of the Holy Spirit.[3] In other words, Solomon is encouraging us to live our lives by the power of the Holy Spirit. The Spirit of the Lord sets us free from the slavery of sin so that we can enjoy the earthly benefits of our salvation in Christ (Rom. 8:1–27). Now that's living!

C. **Enjoy your spouse.** "Enjoy life with the woman whom you love all the days of your fleeting life which He has given to you under the sun; for this is your reward in life, and in your toil in which you have labored under the sun" (Eccles. 9:9). The comforts, delights, and passions of a marital union are to be expressed and relished by each mate. After all, marriage has been sanctioned by God as an honorable relationship, and He considers the marriage bed to be undefiled (Gen. 2:24–25, Matt. 19:4–6, Heb. 13:4). So if you are married, live it up with your spouse! That's what God wants you to do (cf. Song of Solomon).[4]

D. **Throw yourself fully into . . . whatever.** "Whatever your hand finds to do, verily, do it with all your might; for there is no activity or planning or wisdom in Sheol [the grave] where you are going" (Eccles. 9:10). You won't always be able to find pleasure in life, for one day you will die. So don't wait until you retire to enjoy life. Don't even hold back until next week or tomorrow. Start today.

🐟 *Living Insights*

Study One

By now, we can easily identify Solomon's unique writing style. One of his favorite descriptive devices is the use of contrasts—such as righteousness versus wickedness and wisdom versus foolishness.

- Let's take a closer look at our text, Ecclesiastes 9:1–10. After making a copy of the following chart in your notebook, begin listing all the contrasts you can find in these ten verses. In the right column, jot down a statement or two that explain why each contrast is important in this particular context.

3. The biblical case for understanding oil as a symbol of the Holy Spirit's ministry is given by John F. Walvoord in his book *The Holy Spirit,* 3d ed. (Grand Rapids: Zondervan Publishing House, 1981), pp. 21–22.

4. Two excellent commentaries on the Song of Solomon are the following: *A Song for Lovers,* by S. Craig Glickman, foreword by Howard G. Hendricks (Downers Grove: InterVarsity Press, 1976); *Solomon on Sex,* by Joseph C. Dillow (Nashville: Thomas Nelson Publishers, 1977).

Contrasts—Ecclesiastes 9:1–10		
Verses	Contrasting Descriptions	Significance
1		
2		
3		
4		
5		
6		
7		
8		
9		
10		

🐟 *Living Insights*

Study Two

You just don't hear messages like this one very often! When was the last time you heard a preacher tell you to have a blast while you last? Let's take a little test to see how well you're heeding the advice.

- Using the following rating scale, evaluate your personal application of the four responses to life using the number *one* to represent *no application* and *five* for *thorough application*.

Live happily wherever you are.	1	2	3	4	5
Walk in purity and in the power of the Spirit.	1	2	3	4	5
Enjoy your spouse.	1	2	3	4	5
Throw yourself fully into . . . whatever.	1	2	3	4	5

- Based on your scores, which response needs the most work? Jot down two or three ways you can improve your evaluation. Is there a way you can tap into another area of strength in order to provide self-assistance in a weaker area?

An Objective View of the Rat Race
Ecclesiastes 9:11–18

Far too many of us could summarize our lives in three words: *hurry*...
worry... *bury*. Indeed, while most of us are making plans for living, life
is passing us by. Do you feel like you're on a merry-go-round with no way
to get off? Are you beginning to resemble a mouse lost in a futile maze
more than an intelligent human being en route to achieve an admirable
and challenging goal? In Ecclesiastes 9:11–18, Solomon invites us to step
out of the rat race in order to take an honest, objective look at our lives.
He gives us some divine counsel on why we should slow down the pace
and on how we should live out our days.

I. Various Ways to View Life

Before we continue our consideration of the godly outlook on life,
let's look at four popular approaches that are humanistic in
philosophy.

A. Optimism. Those who are optimistic look at life through rose-
colored glasses. They have big dreams and expectations but
ignore reality.

B. Pessimism. This attitude is the opposite of optimism. Pessi-
mists view life as gloomy and humorless. They are convinced
that if something bad can happen, it will. As a result, they often
sneer and seldom express joy.

C. Suspicion. Individuals who are suspicious often border on
being neurotic and paranoid. They think that everyone is out to
get them... that the world is full of cheaters, liars, crooks, and
perverts. Obviously, suspicious people suffer from a lack of trust.
To them, it seems foolish to rely on other people.

D. Fatalism. As we saw in the last lesson, fatalists resign
themselves to accept their lot in life. They feel that since all
events are fixed by forces beyond man's control, human beings
cannot do anything to change what is going to occur. Consequently, their existence becomes a marathon of misery. They
have no hope, only despair.

II. Some Under-the-Sun Counsel

Our study in Ecclesiastes has shown us that Solomon upholds a
realistic approach to life. Optimism, pessimism, suspicion, fatalism... indeed, all other human perspectives fail to present life as it
is. Solomon, however, sets forth the truth about existence and gives
us solid advice on how to fully enjoy it. In the ninth chapter of his
journal, he challenges us not to join others in the unending cycle
of competing harder, running faster, getting up earlier, neglecting
our families, making our jobs a top priority... in short, throwing
ourselves into the rat race without looking back.

A. **The race as it is being run.** Many people want us to believe that the only way to succeed is to be more competitive ... to be stronger, smarter, and faster than the next guy. But Solomon observes that this path usually leads to a dead end. Notice what he writes: "I again saw under the sun that the race is not to the swift, and the battle is not to the warriors, and neither is bread to the wise, nor wealth to the discerning, nor favor to men of ability; for time and chance overtake them all" (Eccles. 9:11). God's sovereign hand has a way of leveling even the best laid plans of the most mighty, clever, and aggressive people on earth (see Dan. 2:20–21, 4:17–37).

B. **The end of all mankind.** Apart from supernatural intervention, the earthly end of every human life is the grave. And unless God reveals otherwise, no individual knows with certainty when his or her life will come to a close. Solomon makes this point clear: "Man does not know his time: like fish caught in a treacherous net, and birds trapped in a snare, so the sons of men are ensnared at an evil time when it suddenly falls on them" (Eccles. 9:12). No matter how resourceful or strong we are, we cannot bypass death. It will halt our plans for success even when we least expect it. In the Book of James, this truth is reiterated with great force:

> Come now, you who say, "Today or tomorrow, we shall go to such and such a city, and spend a year there and engage in business and make a profit." Yet you do not know what your life will be like tomorrow. You are just a vapor that appears for a little while and then vanishes away. Instead, you ought to say, "If the Lord wills, we shall live and also do this or that." (James 4:13–15)

The Lord is in control of our lives. He literally sustains us in existence (Col. 1:17). How foolish it is to think that we can conduct our lives in our own strength, apart from Him! Nothing could be further from the truth.

C. **The nature of those in the race.** To drive his comments home, Solomon gives the example of a wise man who delivered a town from destruction. "There was a small city with few men in it and a great king came to it, surrounded it, and constructed large siegeworks against it. But there was found in it a poor wise man and he delivered the city by his wisdom. Yet no one remembered [or rewarded] that poor man" (Eccles. 9:14–15). Once physical salvation was secured, people continued to pursue success, ignoring the one who had saved them from death. The reaction of these people is sad and unfair. But it is typical of those who are so bent on achieving their own desires and goals that they do not take the time to adequately thank those who have sacrificially given of themselves. In doing so, rat-race participants miss one of the greatest benefits of life—knowing and becoming other-centered.

III. Some Above-the-Sun Wisdom

Based on the verses we have already studied and the few that follow in Ecclesiastes 9, there are five statements of wisdom that rise to the surface. Each one helps us face life realistically and handle it wisely, while reconsidering our involvement in the relentless drive for success.

A. **Human ability cannot guarantee genuine success.** The all-too-common advice of the competitive world is: "Don't push your Christianity too far. Don't allow your sense of right and wrong to keep you from moving up on the corporate ladder. Be tough. Drive hard. Rely on yourself. That's the way to succeed." But this counsel is false (v. 11). God is in control; we are not. Success ultimately comes from His hand, not ours.

B. **Strength is more impressive, yet less effective, than wisdom.** A poor, wise man can deliver a city from the military might of a king. Indeed, wisdom can prevail over strength (vv. 15–16a). However, most people appeal to, and seek after, power while disregarding the insightful counsel of God. Their conduct should not discourage us, but it should help us make a more realistic assessment of those living under the sun.

C. **Wise counsel is never popular, rarely obeyed, and seldom remembered.** As Solomon says, "The wisdom of the poor man is despised and his words are not heeded" (v. 16b). This is true not only in human relationships but also in man's relationship to God. The Holy Spirit is busy convicting " 'the world concerning sin, and righteousness, and judgment' " (John 16:8), but few people ever listen.

D. **Human rulers will always outshout wise counselors, and fools prefer the former.** Many people have the discernment that only comes from God. And when they speak, everyone should listen. Unfortunately, few people ever do (Eccles. 9:17). Most individuals seem to prefer heeding the loudest authority, even when the advice is false, rather than obeying the wise counselor who speaks the truth. If we are wise, we will listen to the quiet voice of truth instead of the bellowing advice of error.

E. **Constructive words of wisdom are no match for destructive weapons of war.** As Solomon puts it, "Wisdom is better than weapons of war, but one sinner destroys much good" (v. 18). A person's foolish, reckless lifestyle can ruin other lives characterized by wisdom. The pursuit of success can drag us down and lead us away from God's Spirit and His Word—our unerring guides for life. So let's step out of the rat race and listen to the Lord as we read His infallible Book. Only then will we begin to experience real success and satisfaction.

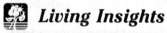 *Living Insights*

Study One

This passage presents us with an honest look at life. It's important to go even further in our study by subjecting ourselves to a series of questions. This exercise will aid us in our appreciation and understanding of the truths found in these verses from Solomon's journal.

- After you copy this chart into your notebook, carefully read Ecclesiastes 9:11–18 and answer the questions listed. Then go back to the passage and look for the answers.

Ecclesiastes 9:11–18	
Questions	Answers
Who?	
What?	
Where?	
When?	
Why?	
How?	

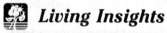 *Living Insights*

Study Two

Let's take a few minutes to analyze your rat race. If you feel the pressure of life's demands, the tension of life's maze, and the fatigue of life's treadmill, this study is for you!

- Take a look back over the last few weeks of your life. As specifically as possible, list the things that have led you into the rat race.
- Now, what is it like to be in the rat race? Describe it in detail.
- How can you bring relief to this lifestyle? Using some of the truths brought out in this study, name some specific things you can begin doing to eliminate the rat-race style of living.

Be Sensible!

Ecclesiastes 10:1–11

In a world rebelling against God, where foolishness reigns and wisdom is ignored, it is all too easy to live our lives from the wrong perspective. None of us are exempt from falling into this trap. We can settle for a lifestyle that displeases the Lord and yields fleeting pleasures and deep dissatisfaction. In fact, the sense of frustration and despair can be so intense that even believers have been known to commit suicide. Is there another option we can take—a better road to travel? Yes, there is, and Solomon shows it to us in the latter chapters of his journal. In Ecclesiastes 10, the king continues calling on us to look above the sun and to seek to live wisely. He spells out his counsel in a series of loosely connected proverbs that contrast the wise and the foolish person. His bottom-line exhortation is, Be sensible! Let's examine the specifics of this counsel in the first eleven verses of chapter 10.

I. A Contrast: Wisdom and Folly

The details of this passage can be grouped under three main categories. Each particular brings us face-to-face with life as it is, and each exhorts us to live wisely rather than foolishly.

A. Advantages versus disadvantages. The first section focuses on the individual. Solomon begins with these words of wisdom: "Dead flies make a perfumer's oil stink, so a little foolishness is weightier than wisdom and honor" (Eccles. 10:1). Just as a few dead flies ruin costly perfume, so a little folly casts a dark shadow over a life otherwise characterized by wisdom and dignity. It is amazing how a person's lapse in good sense can seriously damage his or her reputation. Furthermore, "a wise man's heart directs him toward the right [literally, right hand], but the foolish man's heart directs him toward the left [literally, left hand]" (v. 2). The right hand is commonly used in Scripture as a symbol for protection, power, and the presence of God (cf. Pss. 16:8, 110:5, 121:5–8; Col. 3:1). With this imagery, Solomon is saying that a wise person goes God's way, and in doing so, receives the benefits of a God-centered life. A fool, however, travels in the opposite direction and thereby forfeits the advantages a godly lifestyle brings. Eventually, the habitual refusal to heed God's directives begins to manifest itself in senseless, stupid behavior. Solomon puts it this way: "Even when the fool walks along the road his sense is lacking, and he demonstrates to everyone that he is a fool" (Eccles. 10:3; cf. Prov. 17:12, 18:2, 6). Here, the suggestions for us are simple: Don't waste your energy on a fool. Be wise! Follow God with all your heart.

99

B. Humility and patience versus popularity and partiality. Continuing his counsel, Solomon writes, "If the ruler's temper rises against you, do not abandon your position, because composure allays great offenses" (Eccles. 10:4). Here we are given sound advice on how to handle a hot-headed boss. We might paraphrase it this way: "If your superior becomes angry at you, do not hand in your resignation, because your calm and cool composure can quiet his hot temper." How true this is! And yet, it is so easy for us to return heat with heat, insult with insult, sneer with sneer. What we really need to do is disarm his or her offense with a non-defensive and patient spirit. Another situation Solomon observes is that of incompetent people holding positions of great authority and responsibility. He sees those who are unqualified to lead "set in many exalted places" and "riding on horses" rather than traveling on foot. Meanwhile, individuals who should be in leadership positions are sitting "in humble places" and "walking like slaves on the land" (vv. 6–7). Solomon has in mind here a form of political inequity. Fools are awarded high government positions, while the wise receive civic jobs of limited authority and prestige. Of course, King Solomon is not suggesting that everyone who rises to political prominence is foolish and incompetent. However, he is confronting us with the fact that one's level of skill and discernment does not automatically guarantee a position of equal authority. Rather, other factors—such as popularity, wealth, and friendships—often win people jobs that they are unqualified to perform. Recognition of this phenomenon can help us become more realistic about human government and its limitations.

C. Inevitable risks versus inexcusable stupidity. The last set of contrasts Solomon presents concerns "potential dangers inherent in representative daily tasks ... dangers which could only be averted by applying wisdom or prudence."[1] The situations and dangers given in verses 8–10 can be summarized in the following chart:

Common Situations	Potential Dangers
1. Digging a pit	1. Falling into the pit
2. Breaking through a wall	2. Being bitten by a snake
3. Quarrying stones	3. Being hurt by falling stones
4. Splitting logs	4. Endangering and overexerting oneself due to using a dull axe

1. Donald R. Glenn, "Ecclesiastes," *The Bible Knowledge Commentary: Old Testament Edition,* edited by John F. Walvoord and Roy B. Zuck (Wheaton: Victor Books, 1985), p. 1001.

Of course, fools succumb to these dangers because they fail to exercise good sense. However, Solomon seems to have more in mind here than the obvious. For example, wisdom teaches us that fools will try to dig "pits" for others in an attempt to bring them trouble. But in the process, the foolish end up getting hurt more often than their victims do. Wisdom also instructs us that when fools break through an obstruction in order to, for instance, take advantage of someone else, they set themselves up for being caught or victimized. In short, fools go through life using and abusing other people, often to their own detriment. And yet, the pain fools receive seldom leads to significant changes on their part. Solomon urges us to see the stupidity in this kind of lifestyle and to turn from it by living wisely.

II. Wisdom: Two Marvelous Advantages
In verses 10–11, the insightful writer informs us of two wonderful advantages of wisdom. First, *wisdom prepares the way for success* (v. 10b). Although we might seldom hear this today, it is nonetheless true. Fools may succeed for a season, but in the end their folly will be exposed and they will fail. Second, *wisdom thinks ahead, before the fact.* Unlike a snake charmer who does not take the necessary precautions and therefore is bitten, a wise person plans ahead of a venture, considering the potential dangers so as to take adequate protective measures against them (v. 11).

III. Gaining Wisdom according to Proverbs
How do we gain the wisdom that Solomon is exhorting us to possess and practice? According to James 1:5, we must request that God give it to us: "If any of you lacks wisdom, let him ask of God, who gives to all men generously and without reproach, and it will be given to him." However, prayer is just one step in the process. Proverbs 2:1–4 specifies the other conditions we must fulfill in order to obtain divine wisdom. Carefully consider what it says:

> My son, if you will receive my sayings,
> And treasure my commandments within you,
> Make your ear attentive to wisdom,
> Incline your heart to understanding;
> For if you cry for discernment,
> Lift your voice for understanding;
> If you seek her as silver,
> And search for her as for hidden treasures . . .

In brief, if we strive to understand and heed God's written Word, "then [we] will discern the fear of the Lord, / And discover the knowledge of God." This result will bring us godly wisdom and its many benefits, as verses 6–9 state:

For the Lord gives wisdom;
From His mouth come knowledge and understanding.
He stores up sound wisdom for the upright;
He is a shield to those who walk in integrity,
Guarding the paths of justice,
And He preserves the way of His godly ones.
Then you will discern righteousness and justice
And equity and every good course.

God's wisdom will protect us and give us success. Godly discernment may not be obtained easily, but gaining it is well worth the effort. Are you ready to travel the road of wisdom? God is ready to do His part. He is waiting for you to do yours.

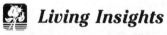 Living Insights

Study One ━━━━━━━━━━━━━━━━━━━━━━━━━━━━━━━━━━━━━━━

Wisdom is produced in our lives through personal teamwork with God. The second chapter of Proverbs provides an excellent example of this team approach. Let's dig into it.

- Copy the following chart into your notebook; then begin reading Proverbs 2. As you work your way through this portion of Scripture, write down commands for you in the first column and gifts from God in the third one. Do this for the first eleven verses and go further, if time permits, by turning to chapter 3.

Wisdom = Teamwork			
Your Part	Verses	God's Part	Verses

Living Insights

Study Two ━━━━━━━━━━━━━━━━━━━━━━━━━━━━━━━━━━━━━━━

Let's do some personal application based on the chart we constructed in study one. We want to be characterized by wisdom, not folly. Let's see how we're doing in this regard.

- As you read over your chart from Proverbs 2, answer this question: Am I keeping up my part of the teamwork? Go through each observation you made and jot down your evaluation next to it.
- Now let's look at the right-hand column. Have you enjoyed any of God's gifts that are listed in Proverbs 2? As you look them over, briefly list the details of your experience with each gift.
- Wrap up this exercise by circling one item in each column that seems to be a weakness in your life. Put together a plan on how to strengthen each item that you circled.

A Fool's Portrait
Ecclesiastes 10:12–20

In our day of diplomacy, straight talk is rare. Many people would rather soft-peddle reality and promote half-truths than communicate the hard facts in a loving way. But the Word of God is different. When it portrays a life, it never glosses over or leaves out the blemishes, scars, or any other imperfections. The divine Artist does not flatter His subjects. He paints them as they are—warts and all. This is clearly evidenced in His portrait of a fool. In the previous lesson we saw that fools do not listen or learn well because they are stubborn in their folly. In this lesson we will learn more about the characteristics of a fool and discover how to deal with one. The picture we will examine is anything but pleasant; indeed, it depicts the tragic and dangerous sides of foolishness. We can be grateful, however, that because God is so loving, He gives us the truth. Let's pay attention to His compassionate, yet realistic, counsel.

I. The Character of a Fool

Before returning to Solomon's journal, it would be helpful to consider some passages from Psalms and Proverbs regarding fools. Among the many things these books say about unwise people, two facts stand out.

A. The language in the fool's heart. Psalm 14:1 says,

The fool has said in his heart, "There is no God."
They are corrupt, they have committed abominable deeds;
There is no one who does good.

A fool is not necessarily a mischievous prankster, a careless blunderer, or an intellectual doubter of the existence of God. Rather, a fool believes there is no God to whom he or she is accountable. Therefore, fools live far below the moral standard of God; they commit atrocities against the Almighty and the people who come into contact with them.

B. The bent of the fool's will. Although all human beings suffer from depravity,[1] fools give in to their sinful wills more completely than others. The Book of Proverbs reveals at least four characteristics of the foolish in this regard. First, *fools traffic in deceit* (Prov. 14:8). They habitually lie with hardly a guilty pang in their conscience. Second, *fools mock sin* (v. 9). They make light of wrongdoing. Sometimes their attitude toward sin emerges in dirty jokes, foul language, or vicious cynicism. But whatever the mode of expression, fools make it clear that they

---

1. A detailed discussion on the meaning and extent of depravity can be found in the study guide titled *Improving Your Serve,* rev. ed., edited by Bill Watkins, from the Bible teaching ministry of Charles R. Swindoll (Fullerton: Insight for Living, 1985), pp. 49–50.

do not consider sin to be sinful. Third, *fools treat wickedness like it is a sport* (10:23, 15:21). They find pleasure in committing sin and exhorting others to do likewise (cf. Rom. 1:32). Fourth, *fools rage against the Lord* (Prov. 19:3). They sneer with malice and vindictiveness at God and His ways. It stands to reason that people with these traits will have difficulty changing their ways. It takes a very stern and severe hand to turn fools toward wisdom.

II. The Actions of a Fool

Now that we have seen what a fool's heart is like, let's turn to Ecclesiastes 10:12–20 to get a God-inspired sketch of his behavior. Here we will learn that there are at least five ways fools manifest their folly.

A. Their harmful verbosity. "Words from the mouth of a wise man are gracious, while the lips of a fool consume him; the beginning of his talking is folly, and the end of it is wicked madness. Yet the fool multiplies words" (vv. 12–14a). In contrast to the wise, whose speech brings them favor and honor, are the foolish, whose talk is self-destructive. The undiscerning multiply words to their own hurt (cf. 5:3, 6:11). Their conversation is foolish from start to finish; it even borders on insanity.

B. Their unpredictable future. Furthermore, fools are ignorant of the fact that "no man knows what will happen, and [no one] can tell him what will come after him" (10:14b). Fools may make elaborate plans for the future or live as if there were no tomorrow, but their rebellious lifestyle renders their fate uncertain. The conduct they choose may land them in the unemployment line, prison, a wheelchair, or even the grave. Only time will tell where their folly will lead them.

C. Their confusion and stupidity. In addition, "the toil of a fool so wearies him that he does not even know how to go to a city" (v. 15). The inefficient and unproductive lifestyle of fools causes them to become so exhausted that they cannot even follow directions. Old Testament scholar Derek Kidner makes some insightful observations concerning Solomon's portrait of a fool:

> The picture begins to emerge of a man who makes things needlessly difficult for himself and for others by his stupidity. And we may need reminding that in the last analysis, this is the thing that could make fools of us all. To be ever learning—never arriving— as 1 Timothy 3:7 portrays some people, is to be a

trifler who contrives to get lost on even the straightest way to the city. That is folly without even the excuse of ignorance.[2]

D. Their destructive leadership. Also, whenever fools are in positions of political authority, the people they govern suffer. Notice what Solomon says: "Woe to you, O land, whose king is a lad and whose princes feast in the morning" (Eccles. 10:16). Solomon is not describing a situation where actual children are ruling. Rather, the writer is depicting a scene where the political leaders are inexperienced, incompetent, and undisciplined (cf. 1 Kings 3:7). A nation that has such people in office is in a sad state of affairs. Israel suffered under these kinds of leaders during various periods in her history. Sometimes, God even elevated fools to leadership positions as judgment on Israel's disobedience. The prophet Isaiah predicted just such an occurrence during his years of ministry. Read carefully what he declared:

For behold, the Lord God of hosts is going to remove
    from Jerusalem and Judah
Both supply and support . . .
The mighty man and the warrior,
The judge and the prophet,
The diviner and the elder,
The captain of fifty and the honorable man,
The counselor and the expert artisan,
And the skillful enchanter.
And I will make mere lads their princes
And capricious children will rule over them,
And the people will be oppressed,
Each one by another, and each one by his neighbor;
The youth will storm against the elder,
And the inferior against the honorable. (Isa. 3:1–5)

How tragic! But little else can be expected from the irresponsible leadership of fools. On the other hand, Solomon says, "Blessed are you, O land, whose king is of nobility and whose princes eat at the appropriate time—for strength, and not for drunkenness" (Eccles. 10:17). Wise leaders are those who have been adequately trained for their positions and possess temperance and discernment in even the most mundane tasks. And the people they govern are considered blessed, for they reap the many benefits of this wise leadership.

E. Their procrastination and poor judgment. This is the last trait of a fool's conduct that Solomon highlights. The

---

2. Derek Kidner, *The Message of Ecclesiastes* (Downers Grove: InterVarsity Press, 1976), p. 93.

Israelite king states it in these words: "Through indolence the rafters sag, and through slackness the house leaks. Men prepare a meal for enjoyment, and wine makes life merry, and money is the answer to everything" (vv. 18–19). What a timely observation! Fools party, waste time, rely too much on money . . . in summary, they lead such careless, undisciplined lives that the essentials of life—like the maintenance of their homes—fall by the wayside.

III. A Warning: Criticism and Confidentiality

Even after viewing Scripture's portrait of a fool, we might think that we can somehow improve our relationship with a fool by discussing it with others. Solomon warns us that such a tack could bring us harm: "In your bedchamber do not curse a [foolish] king, and in your sleeping rooms do not curse a [foolish] rich man, for a bird of the heavens will carry the sound, and the winged creature will make the matter known" (Eccles. 10:20). Living with a fool is one thing, but facing a fool's wrath is quite another. If a fool ever discovers that someone has been confiding with another person concerning his unwise behavior, look out! Fools will retaliate; count on it. Therefore, when we must deal with a fool, confidentiality is often the best approach to take.

IV. A Few Tips on Dealing with a Fool

How, then, should we handle a foolish person? Whether he or she is our mate, friend, minister, employer, or anyone else, the Scriptures specify at least three steps we can take in dealing effectively with a fool.

A. If there is continued folly, isolation is the most effective treatment. Observe the counsel of this proverb: "Leave the presence of a fool, / Or you will not discern words of knowledge" (Prov. 14:7). Some of us may think that this is a terribly harsh response. After all, why not try to reason with a fool? Perhaps he or she will listen and change. The problem with this approach is that it ignores the intensely rebellious nature of a fool; thus, it will not work. Proverbs 23:9 makes this clear: "Do not speak in the hearing of a fool, / For he will despise the wisdom of your words." It is best to separate ourselves from those who persist in living foolishly. This instruction is not supporting divorce from a foolish spouse, but it is suggesting that it is often necessary for the unwise mate to be removed for a time from the benefits of marriage and family. It makes no sense to affirm a foolish marital partner by allowing that spouse to continue in his or her foolishness at home. Unwise mates sometimes need the shock and pain of separation in order to

No matter *Release them from accountability* *Surrender my right for hurting you because you have hurt me.*

shake them from their complacency and confront them with the consequences of their lifestyle.

B. If there is true repentance and brokenness, restoration is appropriate. The process of restoration should begin only when there is solid evidence that a change of heart has occurred in a fool's life. This step is modeled for us by the Lord Himself. Psalm 107 reveals that God does not rush to the rescue of fools. Instead, He causes them to suffer the consequences of their rebellion (Ps. 107:10–12, 39–40). He may even bring them to the brink of despair and death (vv. 17–18). But through this severe treatment, He will frequently gain their attention and promote their repentance. At this point, and not until, the Lord will deliver and heal them (vv. 1–3, 13–14, 19–20). And as He does, so should we.

C. When there is restoration from folly, let there be proclamation. So the psalmist urges:

> Let them [i.e., the restored] give thanks to the Lord
> for His lovingkindness,
> And for His wonders to the sons of men!
> Let them also offer sacrifices of thanksgiving,
> And tell of His works with joyful singing. (vv. 21–22)

Churches need to hear the testimonies of former fools more regularly. Not only will this activity bring glory to God, but it will serve as a reminder to us all of the terrible consequences of foolish living.

Be FIRM in your LOVE

Love must be Tough *Given by Genuine Love + Compassion* *vengeance is only from the Lord*

📖 *Living Insights*

Study One ▬▬▬▬▬▬▬

The twenty verses of Ecclesiastes 10 give tribute to wisdom's excellence and warn of folly's danger. It's a chapter well worth reading again and again.

- Read Ecclesiastes 10:1–20 in your copy of the Scriptures. Then turn to another version of the Word and read these verses once more. If you have the resources available, read the passage in still other translations and paraphrases. This will give you a greater understanding of Solomon's wise counsel.

📖 *Living Insights*

Study Two ▬▬▬▬▬▬▬

This lesson concludes with a few tips on dealing with a fool. Chances are good you may find these suggestions somewhat stretching. So let's

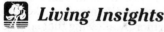 *There must be a God who cares for us so much* *There is a Standard + When I break it there's a price to pay*

go back to the lesson outline. Consult the passages used to support each thought, and fill in the following charts:

If There Is Continued Folly . . . Isolation	
What This Means	What This Does Not Mean

If There Is True Repentance . . . Restoration	
What This Means	What This Does Not Mean

When There Is Restoration . . . Proclamation	
What This Means	What This Does Not Mean

Be Bullish!

Ecclesiastes 11:1–6

"The habit of always putting off an experience until you can afford it, or until the time is right, or until you know how to do it is one of the greatest burglars of joy. Be deliberate, but once you've made up your mind—jump in."[1] Are you in a rut? Have you become a slave to the humdrum activities of your life? When was the last time you broke away from your routine and did something unusual? Have you been told that God wants you to live a dull life? Have unbiblical instruction and well-meaning people robbed you of enjoying life to its fullest? More than likely, most of our answers to these questions would reveal the tedious boredom of our existence. The good news, however, is that we do not have to live this way. The Lord has a much better lifestyle in mind for His people. He wants us to stop existing and start living—in other words, to be *bullish*. This divine plan is embedded in Ecclesiastes 11:1–6. Here we will learn how to leave the ho-hum behind and grab all the gusto life has to offer. Sound great? Let's go for it!

I. Common Human Counsel for the Aging

All too often, the advice handed to us as we grow older prods us to adopt a lifeless lifestyle. For example, some people tell us to stop exerting ourselves and start taking it easy. Others exhort us to avoid risks and live cautiously. Some counselors even encourage us to hold on to what we have because the times are going to get worse and people will try to take advantage of us. But none of these admonitions are supported in Scripture. In Ecclesiastes 11, God shows us the best way to live.

II. God's Uncommon Counsel for All Ages

The last two major sections of Solomon's journal can be summed up in three divinely approved commands: Be bold! Be joyful! Be godly! When these directives are obeyed, they turn a boring life into an exciting and contagious one. In Ecclesiastes 11:1–6, Solomon exhorts us to adopt this lifestyle, to jump into life and experience it to the hilt. He communicates this message through four commands. As we look at each one, we should take special note that God's counsel contradicts much of the human advice we receive today.

A. Instead of protecting, release yourself! This command is implied in these words from Solomon's pen: "Cast your bread on the surface of the waters, for you will find it after many days" (v. 1). We can convey the meaning of verse 1 in this way: "Give of yourself generously, for eventually you will be repaid abundantly." Of course, we may not always receive the kind of

1. Tim Hansel, *When I Relax I Feel Guilty* (Elgin: David C. Cook Publishing Co., 1979), p. 95

return for our generosity that we might expect. But we can look forward to the Lord honoring our vulnerability and service in His way and time.

B. Rather than hoarding, give and invest! As Solomon states it, "Divide your portion to seven, or even to eight, for you do not know what misfortune may occur on the earth" (v. 2). Old Testament scholar Walter Kaiser explains this text well. Observe what he says:

> "Be liberal and generous to as *many* as you can and *then some*," is the way we would say it. So, make as many friends as you can, for you never know when you yourself may need assistance. Instead of becoming miserly just because you fear that the future may hold some evil reversal of your fortunes, leaving you in poverty and want, you should all the more distribute to as many as possible so that you can have the blessing of receiving in the event of such reverses.[2]

This passage is not the only one in Scripture that promises a return on our investments. For example, Proverbs 19:17 says, "He who is gracious to a poor man lends to the Lord, / And He will repay him for his good deed." The God who cannot fail promises that He will faithfully recompense whatever we give. On the other hand, Proverbs 21:13 states, "He who shuts his ear to the cry of the poor / Will also cry himself and not be answered." If we hoard rather than give, ignore needs instead of meet them, then we will not be heard when we request assistance.

C. In place of drifting, pursue! This command is inferred from a passage that seems enigmatic at first. But when we consider it in light of Ecclesiastes 1:3–10, where the emphasis is on the wearisome and humanly unalterable cycles of nature, we can get a handle on its meaning. "If the clouds are full, they pour out rain upon the earth; and whether a tree falls toward the south or toward the north, wherever the tree falls, there it lies. He who watches the wind will not sow and he who looks at the clouds will not reap" (11:3–4). The happenings described in these verses are inevitable and predictable. Full clouds will give rain, falling trees will lie where they land, and people who spend their time watching the weather will not produce anything of value. By mentioning such occurrences, Solomon probably has in mind individuals who waste their time and energy observing the obvious, talking about the inevitable, and

2. Walter Kaiser, *Ecclesiastes: Total Life* (Chicago: Moody Press, 1979), p. 114.

worrying about both. What profit is there in living one's life this way? There is none. How much better it is to be pursuing life rather than watching it pass by, to be working on the things that we can change rather than worrying about those things that we cannot alter in the least! Solomon is exhorting us to get down from the spectators' stands and run onto the playing field. We have nothing to lose and everything to gain by taking his advice.

D. As an alternative to doubting, trust! Solomon's final piece of counsel in this section is embedded in these verses:

> Just as you do not know the path of the wind and how bones are formed in the womb of the pregnant woman, so you do not know the activity of God who makes all things. Sow your seed in the morning, and do not be idle in the evening, for you do not know whether morning or evening sowing will succeed, or whether both of them alike will be good. (vv. 5–6)

There are a number of things in life that we do not fully understand—such as the nature and work of the infinite God. But many people will not launch into anything until they grasp it fully and rid it of all risks. How few things we could do if we adopted this approach to life! Solomon rightly urges us to throw this philosophy to the wind. In its place, he calls on us to live life to the fullest, trusting God along the way. Why? Because we do not know which activities we engage in will bring an abundant return. We need to go for it and not look back! God will honor our efforts.

III. For Those Who Dare to Be Bullish

As we wrap up our study of this section from Solomon's ancient diary, let's consider three challenges that can help us become bullish in our approach to life.

A. Start living it up today and never quit. Let's invest time in someone, volunteer ourselves for service, and refuse to allow our lives to collect dust.

B. Remember that wisdom must accompany action. We need to be careful not to rush out unprepared in our zeal to plunge into life. Certainly, we need to get out and get going, but we should do it with godly discernment.

C. Watch out for enemy attacks during lulls in the action. When we set out to boldly live for Jesus Christ, we ought to expect that times of little excitement and low productivity will come. It is often during these periods that we are prompted by others to entertain doubts regarding the value of living a bold Christian life. However, aggressive living is threatening to those who refuse to live that way. Remembering this will help keep us from giving in to mediocrity and will motivate us to press on with enthusiasm. So what are we waiting for? Let's start living!

 Living Insights

Study One ■■■■■■■■■■■■■■■■■■■■■■■■■■■■■■■■■■■■■■■

It has been suggested that the final two chapters of Ecclesiastes could be reduced to three commands totaling six words: Be bold! Be joyful! Be godly! Let's spend a few minutes on each topic. Copy the following chart into your notebook and write in Scripture passages, biblical characters, and/or situations from the Word that correspond to each command. You may be surprised at how much Scripture has to say about each of these areas of living!

Boldness in the Bible
Joy in the Scriptures
Godliness in God's Word

Continued on next page

Boldness, joy, and godliness—these are important traits for the Christian. If you were to ask your closest friend whether or not these traits characterize *your* life, what sort of answer do you think you would receive? Let's find out.

- Set up a time to meet with your closest friend. It may be a mate, a brother or sister, or someone else who knows you well. While you are together, ask this individual to speak candidly about his or her perceptions of you as a person of boldness, joy, and godliness. Be ready for the straight scoop. If weaknesses are exposed, ask him or her to suggest how these areas could be strengthened. By the way, don't forget to thank this individual for his or her input.

Enjoying Life Now, Not Later

Ecclesiastes 11:7–12:1

Do you enjoy who you are and what you have? Or has your life become an endurance test full of frowns, whines, groans, and sighs? If you answered yes to the first question, you are among the fortunate few. Unfortunately, the second question more accurately describes life for the vast majority. While many people may have occasional good times that bring smiles and laughter into their lives, their joy is quickly lost amidst a sea of disappointment, frustration, anxiety, and resentment. Lasting happiness seems to be at best an elusive reality. But many individuals still try to find it, hoping that in time some thing, some person, or some event will make them happy. In this lesson we will explore several ways people attempt to find joy. Our investigation may yield a few surprising conclusions, but the end result will be some sound counsel on how to be both presently and eternally happy.

I. What Are We Waiting For?

If we were to ask various individuals "What are you waiting for in order to enjoy life? " we would probably get one of three typical answers. Some people would respond by saying, "I will be happy when I have all the things I've ever wanted." But Jesus Christ warns us that material possessions will not bring joy: " 'Beware, and be on your guard against every form of greed; for not even when one has an abundance does his life consist of his possessions' " (Luke 12:15). Author John Gardner reiterates this truth in some biting words that are directly addressed to Americans but indirectly applicable to anyone who seeks satisfaction in wealth: "If happiness could be found in having material things, and in being able to indulge yourself in things that you consider pleasurable, then we, in America, would be deliriously happy. We would be telling one another frequently of our unparalleled bliss, rather than trading tranquilizer prescriptions."[1] Another answer to our question would go something like this: "I will be happy when I meet the person who will fulfill my life." This response might come from a single person looking for a spouse, a married couple anxious to have their first baby, or even a lonely individual longing for a close friend. Whatever the case, the Scriptures repeatedly illustrate that we cannot depend on other people for our happiness. Even close friends and family members can disappoint and hurt us (see 2 Sam. 13:30–39, 16:11–12; Job 2:7–10, 19:13–19; Pss. 41:7–9, 55:12–14). Yet another response numerous individuals would give is, "I will be happy when I have achieved my goals and realized my dreams." Solomon, however, demonstrates

---

1. John Gardner, *Self-Renewal* (New York: W. W. Norton and Co., 1981), as quoted by Tim Hansel in *When I Relax I Feel Guilty* (Elgin: David C. Cook Publishing Co., 1979), p. 109.

throughout Ecclesiastes that this path will never lead to genuine contentment. Besides, James tells us in his epistle that we can find joy even through the often painful process of completing our goals in Christ (James 1:2–4). So how can we begin to experience lasting happiness now? Let's turn to Solomon's divinely inspired journal and find out.

II. What Does Solomon Say about Enjoying Life?

As we will quickly discover, Solomon links our joy with our relationship to God. Let's delve into what he says.

A. We are given permission to enjoy life. Solomon gives us the first part of his answer as to how we can enjoy life in these words: "The light is pleasant, and it is good for the eyes to see the sun" (Eccles. 11:7). In Scripture, light and sunshine are frequently used to represent the warmth and security of God's love (see Ps. 27:1a, Isa. 60:20, Micah 7:8). Solomon employs this imagery to say that it is good for us to rest in God's loving protection. When we do this, we will realize that He accepts us and desires that we enjoy our lives. To make certain that we do not miss this fact, Solomon writes, "Indeed, if a man should live many years, let him rejoice in them all" (Eccles. 11:8a). We don't have to wait to enjoy life; we can begin living it up now!

B. All the traditional limitations have been removed. Some people declare that the time to appreciate life is during our youth. Others insist that because young people have many difficult adjustments to make, the best time to find happiness is when we are independent of our parents and "in touch" with our own identities. But Solomon challenges both of these common claims. He exhorts us to rejoice in all the years we spend on earth (v. 8a). He even talks specifically to the young person: "Rejoice, young man, during your childhood, and let your heart be pleasant during the days of young manhood. *And follow the impulses of your heart and the desires of your eyes*" (v. 9a, emphasis added). Now that's definitely non-traditional counsel!

C. God inserts just enough warnings to keep us obedient. Lest we turn our liberty into a license to sin, the merciful Lord adds some warnings through Solomon's words. After encouraging us to enjoy all our years (v. 8a), the writer exhorts us to "remember the days of darkness, for they shall be many" (v. 8b). Tough times will come—periods marked by pain, disappointment, struggle, and sorrow. But they need not disillusion us and steal our joy (cf. Matt. 5:10–12; James 1:2–4, 12, 5:11). If we know that some dark days will enter our lives, then we can better prepare for them in a way that will deepen our happiness rather than destroy it. To this instruction, Solomon adds that we should temper the exercise of our liberty by realizing "that God will bring [us] to judgment" for our actions (Eccles. 11:9b). The Lord will hold us accountable for all that we think, say, and do (Matt. 12:36–37, 16:27; 2 Cor. 5:10). Thus, we should use our freedom for good ends, not for evil. And as we do what is right, God will increase our joy (Prov. 4:18, 10:6, 28, 14:14, 22; Matt. 5:6). Another warning Solomon gives is this: "Remove vexation from your heart and put away pain from your body, because childhood and the prime of life are fleeting" (Eccles. 11:10). The Hebrew term for *vexation* combines two ideas—anger and resentment. When these coexist in a person's life, there is rebellion. In other words, we are being warned to rid our lives of a rebellious spirit. Alongside this exhortation comes yet another—to get rid of those things that give us physical pain. These pain-producers may be drugs, alcohol, tobacco, or even illicit sex. Whatever they are, we need to put them out of our lives if we want to live happily.

D. The all-inclusive, essential ingredient for happiness is a vital relationship with God. Finally, after chapters filled with dissatisfaction and despair, Solomon tells us the necessary ingredient for experiencing joy in our lives now. What is it? "Remember [i.e., act decisively in favor of] ... your Creator in the days of your youth, before the evil days come and the years draw near when you will say, 'I have no delight in them' " (Eccles. 12:1). Put another way, our happiness is directly linked to our obedience to God. When we submit to His Word through faith in Jesus Christ, we will begin experiencing the Lord's abundant blessings.

III. What Hinders the Pursuit of Happiness?

Now that we know how we can be happy, we should briefly look at two barriers that threaten our daily joy.

A. Self-appointed excuses keep us from claiming daily joy. "If only so-and-so were different ... If only I lived somewhere else ... If only I had more money ... If my children would obey me better ... If my mate showed me more affection"—the list of excuses goes on and on. We don't have to wait for our circumstances to change. We can find pleasure in our lives right now (Phil. 4:11–13).

B. Self-styled independence keeps us from remembering our Creator. "I'll make it on my own. I don't need God or anyone else. I know where I am going and how I want to get there." These are familiar words in our day, but the attitude they convey robs us of true happiness. Why? Because it keeps us from relying on the only One who can give us lasting joy—the loving Lord. If you have not committed your life to Him, will you do so today? And if you have already claimed Him as your Savior, will you commit yourself to serving Him faithfully?

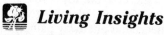 *Living Insights*

Study One

As we approach the conclusion of Solomon's journal, we arrive at some long-awaited words concerning the Lord. Let's make certain we know what Solomon is saying in this passage.

- Once you've reread Ecclesiastes 11:7–12:1, make a copy of the chart given below. There are a number of words in this passage that are keys to understanding the text. Write them in the left column and begin defining their meanings based on the immediate context and any other relevant Scriptures you find. Finally, consult a Bible dictionary for further help and information.

Ecclesiastes 11:7–12:1		
Key Words	Verses	Definitions

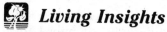 *Living Insights*

Study Two

When you summarize the art of enjoying life, you will face a few key questions. The following three ought to prompt you to do some real reflection on personal joy.

- What excuses am I using that keep me from claiming daily joy?
- What areas of my life have been affected by self-styled independence, thus keeping me from remembering the Creator?
- What do I need to do in order to enjoy life now?

Gray Hairs, Fewer Teeth,
Yet a Big Smile
Ecclesiastes 12:1–8

Every tick of the clock, each new sunrise, and every passing year is a reminder that each of us is growing older. None of us can alter the progression of time, though some of us may try to ignore it. Thus, the question for us is not "How can we stop aging?" but "How can we age with grace and a sense of worth?" Can we grow older and yet continue to live purposefully and happily? Can we enter our twilight years excited about new challenges rather than weighed down with regrets? The answers to these and other questions can be found in Ecclesiastes 12:1–8. This passage presents a realistic picture of the aging process and couples it with some down-to-earth advice. So let's listen attentively as a wise, elderly king shares with us the secret of growing old with grace.

I. Some Traditional Feelings among the Aged

We will appreciate Solomon's counsel more fully once we have surveyed some feelings commonly shared among the elderly. Some older people think that they are simply in everybody's way. This sense of *uselessness* is prominent among those who were once very resourceful and highly respected. Other elderly people wish that they could live their lives over. These individuals feel *guilty* about what might or should have been. Still others age with a sense of *bitterness* and *resentment.* They feel that life handed them a raw deal. Anger over this frequently leads to *self-pity.* Another common feeling among the elderly is intensified *fear.* They are often afraid of such things as bankruptcy, heights, ill health, death, loneliness, and senility. Certainly, growing older has its difficulties. And all too frequently, those who are younger do not make life easier and more enjoyable for those getting on in years. But do all these negative feelings have to accompany us as we age? What does God's Word have to say about getting older? Let's find out.

II. A Divine Perspective Worth Considering

Ecclesiastes 12 is a beacon of light in a book that illustrates the darkness of life apart from God. In this final chapter, the author calls us to "remember ... [our] Creator in the days of [our] youth, before the evil days come and the years draw near when [we] will say, 'I have no delight in them'" (v. 1). Derek Kidner writes that "to remember [the Creator] is no perfunctory or purely mental act: it is to drop our pretense of self-sufficiency and to commit ourselves to Him."[1] And we are exhorted to do this while we are young. But why not wait until we are older to submit ourselves to the Lord and

1. Derek Kidner, *The Message of Ecclesiastes* (Downers Grove: InterVarsity Press, 1976), p. 100.

His ways? Because, says Solomon, our investment in evil rather than good will pay dreadful dividends. It will lead to scars, heartaches, and regrets that we will carry into our old age. This sorrow and guilt will steal our peace and joy not only now but also in the years to come. Besides, the aging process involves enough difficult changes without adding the detrimental consequences of an ungodly lifestyle. Solomon describes many of these trying adjustments with some eloquent imagery. Let's observe what he says.

A. **Mental dullness and depression.** As we grow older, there will come a time when "the sun, the light, the moon, and the stars are darkened, and clouds return after the rain" (v. 2). In other words, we will eventually think less clearly and remember less accurately. And as our mental abilities begin to deteriorate, we will grow increasingly depressed over their decline.

B. **Physical ailments and limitations.** Not only will our minds begin to fail but so will our bodies. Solomon brings this fact to light rather graphically. The phrase "in the day that the watchmen of the house tremble" refers to the involuntary shaking of an older person's head, voice, and hands (v. 3a). When Solomon says "and mighty men stoop," he has in mind legs that have become bent and feeble (v. 3b). As we age, our "grinding ones stand idle because they are few" (v. 3c). That is, our teeth become fewer in number and thereby make it harder for us to consume our food. Our "windows [also] grow dim" (v. 3d). It becomes more difficult for us to see clearly. Furthermore, we soon find that "the doors on the street are shut as the sound of the grinding mill is low" (v. 4a). These words may refer to either a decreased ability to hear or the sinking in of one's lips due to the loss of teeth.[2] To this, Solomon adds that the elderly "arise at the sound of the bird" (v. 4b). Their increased inability to sleep causes them to awake earlier than when they were young. Older people also either hear songs more faintly because of their impaired hearing or sing more softly because their voices are not as strong as they used to be (v. 4c).[3] In addition, old age often brings a fear of high places "and of terrors on the road" (v. 5a). The phrase "the almond tree blossoms" speaks of hair turning gray or white (v. 5b), and "the grasshopper drags himself along" refers to the slower movement of the elderly (v. 5c). Eventually, even "the caperberry" will become "ineffective"—that is, the ability to procreate will be lost (v. 5d).

2. Donald R. Glenn, "Ecclesiastes," *The Bible Knowledge Commentary: Old Testament Edition,* edited by John F. Walvoord and Roy B. Zuck (Wheaton: Victor Books, 1985), p. 1005.

3. Donald R. Glenn, "Ecclesiastes," *The Bible Knowledge Commentary: Old Testament Edition,* p. 1005.

C. Life's final factor. At this juncture, Solomon returns to his opening command but gives us a new motive for obeying it. Rather than focusing on the consequences we must face should we ignore this directive (v. 1), he exhorts us to live for God in light of our approaching death: "Remember Him before the silver cord is broken and the golden bowl is crushed, the pitcher by the well is shattered and the wheel at the cistern is crushed; then the dust will return to the earth as it was, and the spirit will return to God who gave it" (vv. 6–7). To this the Book of Hebrews adds a theme that occurs throughout Ecclesiastes: "It is appointed for men to die once and after this comes judgment" (Heb. 9:27; cf. Eccles. 3:17, 11:9, 12:14). If we have accepted Jesus Christ as our Savior before we die, then our life beyond death will be more exhilarating than we could ever imagine (Rev. 21:1–22:5). However, if we die before placing our faith in the Messiah, then our earthly life will have been lived in vain (Eccles. 12:8), and our life beyond will be one of torment in hell (Matt. 8:11–12, 13:49–50; Luke 16:22–28; 2 Thess. 1:8–9; Rev. 20:10–15). This is not a pleasant thought, but it is nonetheless the truth.

III. Some Practical Advice between the Lines
As we reflect on Solomon's comments about aging and our relationship to God, we can discern at least three thoughts that are communicated between the lines.
A. We must face the fact that we are not getting any younger. Ignoring old age will not make it go away. Aging is an inevitable reality of life that we all need to face.
B. God has designed us to be empty without Him. Our hearts will find no rest and our souls no peace until we place our lives in His loving hands.
C. Now is the time to prepare for eternity. Preparing for retirement is commendable. But it's all for nothing if we have not made adequate plans to spend forever with God. The Lord wants us to entrust our lives to Him so that we can enjoy His presence endlessly. But He will not force us against our wills. As C. S. Lewis says,

> "There are only two kinds of people in the end: those who say to God, 'Thy will be done,' and those to whom God says, in the end, '*Thy* will be done.' All that are in Hell, choose it. Without that self-choice there could be no Hell. No soul that seriously and constantly desires joy will ever miss it. Those who seek find. To those who knock it is opened."[4]

4. C. S. Lewis, *The Great Divorce* (New York: Macmillan Publishing Co., 1946), pp. 72–73.

📖 Living Insights

We've turned the page to the final chapter of Solomon's journal. This is a good time to think back over the previous studies. Let's review some of the highlights together.

- The following chart lists the titles for the first twelve lessons. Flip back through the pages of your study guide and notebook in order to discover the most meaningful truth and the most helpful application you found in each lesson. Write them down in the appropriate columns.

Living on the Ragged Edge		
Lessons	Truths	Applications
Journal of a Desperate Journey		
Chasing the Wind		
Eat, Drink, . . . and Be *What?*		
More Miles of Bad Road		
Do You Know What Time It Is?		
Interlude of Rare Insight		
Confessions of a Cynic		
The Lonely Whine of the Top Dog		
One Plus One Equals Survival		
What Every Worshiper Should Remember		
Straight Talk to the Money-Mad		
The Few Years of a Futile Life		

📖 Living Insights

Study one provided the opportunity to reflect on the first half of the lessons on Ecclesiastes. Let's continue in the same way by reviewing the last half of this series.

- Once again, duplicate the following chart in your notebook. As you look over the last several lessons, pinpoint one truth and one application that was especially significant to you.

Living on the Ragged Edge		
Lessons	Truths	Applications
Wise Words for Busy People		
Putting Wisdom to Work		
The Qualities of a Good Boss		
Mysteries That Defy Explanation		
Have a Blast While You Last!		
An Objective View of the Rat Race		
Be Sensible!		
A Fool's Portrait		
Be Bullish!		
Enjoying Life Now, Not Later		
Gray Hairs, Fewer Teeth, Yet a Big Smile		

Wrapping Up a Ragged-Edge Journey

Ecclesiastes 12:8–14

Most of us assume that philosophers will wrestle with the basic issues of life. We even allow scientists and university professors to end their experiments and lectures with question marks rather than exclamation points. But what about preachers? Do we expect them to struggle with cherished beliefs? Do we permit them to entertain doubts, to challenge some of our most basic assumptions about life, to rebel against the status quo? In many circles, no such leeway is granted to ministers. Indeed, their confessed disillusionments and frustrations frequently send shock waves through the communities they serve. And yet, it is unrealistic for us to expect ministers to have all the answers. The Lord even saw fit to remind us of this fact by inspiring and preserving the ragged-edge journey of one ancient preacher, King Solomon. And, as we have seen, his search for satisfaction and meaning has no limit to its application. In a very real sense his pursuit is our own. We may not have understood this when we began studying his journal, but by now there is no question regarding the relevance of his words to our lives. So as we meditate on the last few verses of Ecclesiastes, let's allow the Preacher's conclusion to do its life changing work.

I. The Preacher's Central Thesis

Solomon never leaves us in doubt concerning the major proposition he expounds and defends. He states it in the opening remarks of chapter 1: " 'Vanity of vanities,' says the Preacher, / 'Vanity of vanities! All is vanity' " (Eccles. 1:2). As he develops his case by giving example after example of the emptiness of life apart from God, he uses the Hebrew term for *vanity* no less than thirty times. Why does he think that this position needs to be developed so thoroughly or even addressed at all? Because he recognizes that it raises one of the most significant questions that any human being could pose—namely, If life has no purpose or meaning, then why go on working or even living? (v. 3). Of course, many people ignore this issue rather than face it. They continue to search for meaning to their lives apart from a faith-commitment in God. These individuals are like the man described in Stephen Crane's poem

> I saw a man pursuing the horizon;
> Round and round they sped.
> I was disturbed at this;
> I accosted the man.
> "It is futile," I said,

"You can never—"
"You lie," he cried,
And ran on.[1]

Other people try to bravely accept the futility of existence without
God. Atheist Albert Camus supports this position with these words:

> The absurd man ... catches sight of a burning and frigid,
> transparent and limited universe in which nothing is
> possible but everything is given, and beyond which all is
> collapse and nothingness. He can then decide to accept
> such a universe and draw from it his strength, his refusal
> to hope, and the unyielding evidence of a life without
> consolation.[2]

Still others decide that since their lives have no purpose, they might
as well end them. But even suicide does not always offer relief for
those in despair. Consider these bleak comments from the pen of
atheist Jean-Paul Sartre:

> I dreamed vaguely of killing myself to wipe out at least
> one of these superfluous lives. But even my death would
> have been *In the way. In the way,* my corpse, my blood
> on these stones, between those plants, at the back of this
> smiling garden. And the decomposed flesh would have
> been *In the way* in the earth which would receive my
> bones, at last, cleaned, stripped, peeled, proper and clean
> as teeth, it would have been *In the way;* I was *In the way*
> for eternity.[3]

So the question remains, How can we find purpose and joy under
the sun? By looking above the sun to our Creator and Redeemer ...
by obeying Him even "in the days of [our] youth" (12:1). There is a
cure for despair; it is found through faith in the Son of God, Jesus
Christ (John 3:16).

II. The Preacher's Closing Confession

As Solomon brings his journal to a close, he records the end of his
arduous journey. And so the reader does not forget the primary
thesis, Solomon repeats it one last time: " 'Vanity of vanities,' says
the Preacher, 'all is vanity!' " (Eccles. 12:8). We dare not try to evade
this truth. Without God at its center, life is empty. The Preacher goes
on to share with us his personal understanding of his craft, and he
attaches a pertinent warning for all to heed.

. Stephen Crane, from *The Black Riders and Other Lines,* as quoted by James Sire in *The
Universe Next Door: A Basic World View Catalog* (Downers Grove: InterVarsity Press, 1976),
p. 86–87.

. Albert Camus, *The Myth of Sisyphus and Other Essays* (New York: Vintage Press, 1955), p. 44.

. Jean-Paul Sartre, *Nausea* (New York: New Directions, 1959), p. 173.

A. Solomon's approach to preaching. Solomon states, "In addition to being a wise man, the Preacher also taught the people knowledge; and he pondered, searched out and arranged many proverbs. The Preacher sought to find delightful words and to write words of truth correctly" (vv. 9–10). It is of primary importance that the minister be a man characterized by godly wisdom. He is also expected to instruct people in the truth. But even truth can be communicated in a boring, ineffective manner. Thus, a pastor should seek out just the right words and method of delivery so that God's Word penetrates lives clearly, practically, and powerfully. As Bible scholar J. B. Phillips once said, "If words are to enter men's hearts and bear fruit, they must be the right words shaped cunningly to pass men's defenses and explode silently and effectually within their minds."[4] Can a well-prepared sermon delivered by a godly preacher really accomplish all this? Solomon says yes. Notice what he writes: "The words of wise men are like goads, and masters of these collections are like well-driven nails; they are given by one Shepherd" (v. 11). The wisely chosen words of a preacher can guide and stimulate others toward godly living. His sermons can even drive the truth into someone's life so as to give him a secure basis for living that he will not forget. This happens when a minister is diligent in sermon preparation and cooperates with the divine Shepherd in sermon delivery. Such a team approach allows God to speak through the words of the preacher as he faithfully and accurately expounds the Lord's Word. Now that's a combination that can't lose! (Isa. 55:11)

B. Solomon's warning to all. "Beyond this," adds Solomon, "be warned: the writing of many books is endless, and excessive devotion to books is wearying to the body" (Eccles. 12:12). When we recall that this warning was written during a period without printing presses, word processors, and computers, it becomes even more significant. Each year thousands of new books are published, and countless pieces of information are stored in filing cabinets and computer banks. No human being on earth has the time or energy to search through these materials for solutions to the enigmas and problems of life. Fortunately, we do not need to resort to such a task. The Lord has given us the answers we need to the most fundamental questions of life and He has brought them together into one book—the Bible (2 Tim. 3:16–17). Therefore, His Word should be our primary authoritative guide for living.

---

4. J. B. Phillips, as quoted by Charles R. Swindoll in *Living on the Ragged Edge: Coming to Terms with Reality* (Waco: Word Books, 1985), p. 368.

III. Let's Consider the Conclusion

Solomon's conclusion is simple and to the point: "Fear God and keep His commandments, because this applies to every person" (Eccles. 12:13). Why are these commands relevant to all? Because "God will bring every act to judgment, everything which is hidden, whether it is good or evil" (v. 14; cf. Matt. 10:26). God is the answer to our despair, and obedience to Him is the cure for our dissatisfaction. We can choose to believe or deny what He says. But all of us will one day have to face Him and give an account of our lives. No one will escape His judgment, and no one will receive everlasting bliss apart from personal faith in Christ (John 11:25–26, 14:6; Acts 4:10–12). Are you ready to stand before the Creator, the impartial Judge of all? If so, inexpressible joy will be yours forever. However, if you are unprepared to face the living God, start putting your life in order today. The Lord is waiting to give you His best. But first you must give Him your life (John 12:24–26, Rom. 6:3–11).

Living Insights

Study One

Solomon develops Ecclesiastes like a good mystery writer. He makes us wait until the last chapter before giving us the answers to many of the questions that popped into our minds as we read the book! But at last we have arrived at the conclusion.

- Ecclesiastes 12:8–14 is unquestionably the key passage in the entire book. Take a careful look at these seven verses, and rewrite them in your own words. Think of this as an expanded paraphrase intended to highlight the meanings of important terms. This will be time well spent toward clarifying and personalizing the text.

Living Insights

Study Two

As we close our study of Ecclesiastes, it's possible for us to have notebooks filled with good notes but no real nuggets of truth in our hearts and minds. So let's conclude with a valuable, lasting lesson.

- Ecclesiastes 12:13–14 summarizes one of the most significant themes in all Scripture. Write these two verses down on an index card and begin the simple process of committing these words to memory. Read the verses aloud several times, and you'll begin to see how quickly and easily they stay with you. One last thing: the key to memory-work retention is *review.* The more you review these verses, the deeper they will become ingrained in your life.

127

Books for Probing Further

Solomon is right—an "excessive devotion to books *is* wearying to the body" (Eccles. 12:12b, emphasis added). However, we would be amiss if we understood this comment as an exhortation to read nothing but the Bible. Certainly, much of our reading and meditating time should be spent in the Scriptures. But even the biblical writers never instruct God's people to study the Word exclusively. Indeed, the prophets and apostles frequently quote from or allude to sections of extra-biblical literature in order to communicate their messages (for example, see Matt. 5:21–45, Acts 17:28b, Titus 1:12). Thus, Solomon's statement should be understood as a warning not to exhaust ourselves by trying to read everything available. Instead, we should focus our study on those resources that can broaden and illumine our understanding of God, His works, and His relationship to creation. In other words, our extra-biblical reading should supplement, not replace, our study of God's Word and interaction with His creation. With this in mind, we have selected some books that can increase your knowledge and application of several topics that are addressed in this study guide. We hope that you will use them wisely, testing everything they say in light of the clear teaching of Scripture (Acts 17:11).

I. Coming to Terms with Wisdom

Cameron, Jocelyn E., comp. *Words to the Wise.* Foreword by Bruce K. Waltke Langley: Credo Publishing Co., 1984.

God's Wisdom for Daily Reading. Nashville: Thomas Nelson Publishers, 1984

Ironside, Henry Allan. *Notes on the Book of Proverbs.* New York: Loizeaux Brothers, n.d.

Kidner, Derek. *The Proverbs: An Introduction and Commentary.* The Tyndale Old Testament Commentaries. Downers Grove: InterVarsity Press, 1964

Kidner, Derek. *The Wisdom of Proverbs, Job and Ecclesiastes: An Introduction to Wisdom Literature.* Downers Grove: InterVarsity Press, 1985.

Mayhall, Carole. *Lord, Teach Me Wisdom: One Woman's Search.* Colorado Springs: NavPress, 1979.

II. Coming to Terms with Joy

Arthur, Kay. *How Can I Be Blessed.* Old Tappan: Fleming H. Revell Co., 1985

Butterworth, Bill. *Peanut Butter Families Stick Together.* Introduction by Chuck Swindoll. Old Tappan: Fleming H. Revell Co., 1985.

Chapian, Marie. *Staying Happy in an Unhappy World.* Old Tappan: Fleming H. Revell Co., 1985.

DeKruyter, Arthur H. *Journey into Joy.* Old Tappan: Fleming H. Revell Co. 1985.

Gordon, Arthur. *A Touch of Wonder.* Old Tappan: Fleming H. Revell Co., 1974

Hansel, Tim. *When I Relax I Feel Guilty.* Elgin: David C. Cook Publishing Co 1979.

Johnston, Robert K. *The Christian at Play.* Grand Rapids: William B Eerdmans Publishing Co., 1983.

Kaiser, Walter. *Ecclesiastes: Total Life.* Chicago: Moody Press, 1979

Kidner, Derek. *The Message of Ecclesiastes.* Downers Grove: InterVarsity Press, 1976.

MacDonald, Gordon. *Ordering Your Private World.* Nashville: Thomas Nelson Publishers, 1984.

Mayhall, Carole. *Filled to Overflowing.* Colorado Springs: NavPress, 1984.

Morrice, William G. *Joy in the New Testament.* Foreword by A. M. Hunter. Grand Rapids: William B. Eerdmans Publishing Co., 1984.

Stedman, Ray C. *Solomon's Secret: Enjoying Life, God's Good Gift.* Portland: Multnomah Press, 1985.

Swindoll, Charles R. *Living on the Ragged Edge: Coming to Terms with Reality.* Waco: Word Books, 1985.

Watson, Thomas. *The Beatitudes: An Exposition of Matthew 5:1–12.* Reprint. Carlisle: The Banner of Truth Trust, 1980.

III. Coming to Terms with Non-Christian Philosophies

Bloesch, Donald G. *Crumbling Foundations: Death and Rebirth in an Age of Upheaval.* Grand Rapids: Academie Books, Zondervan Publishing House, 1984.

Evans, C. Stephen. *Existentialism: The Philosophy of Despair and the Quest for Hope.* With a response by William Lane Craig. Rev. ed. Christian Free University Curriculum. Grand Rapids: Zondervan Publishing House; Richardson: Probe Ministeries International, 1984.

Geisler, Norman L. *The Creator in the Courtroom: "Scopes II."* With A. F. Brooke II and Mark J. Keough. Milford: Mott Media, 1982.

Geisler, Norman L. *False Gods of Our Time.* Eugene: Harvest House Publishers, 1985.

Geisler, Norman L. *Is Man the Measure? An Evaluation of Contemporary Humanism.* Grand Rapids: Baker Book House, 1983.

Geisler, Norman L., and Amano, J. Yutaka. *Religion of the Force.* Dallas: Quest Publications, P. O. Box 38100, 1983.

Geisler, Norman L., and Watkins, William D. *Perspectives: Understanding and Evaluating Today's World Views.* San Bernardino: Here's Life Publishers, Inc., 1984.

Goudzwaard, Bob. *Idols of Our Time.* Translated by Mark Vander Vennen. Foreword by Howard A. Snyder. Downers Grove: InterVarsity Press, 1984.

Gundry, Stanley N., and Johnson, Alan F., eds. *Tensions in Contemporary Theology.* Rev. ed. Foreword by Roger Nicole. Chicago: Moody Press, 1976.

Hackett, Stuart C. *Oriental Philosophy: A Westerner's Guide to Eastern Thought.* Madison: The University of Wisconsin Press, Ltd., 1979.

Kirk, J. Andrew. *Liberation Theology: An Evangelical View from the Third World.* New Foundations Theological Library. Atlanta: John Knox Press, 1979.

Machen, J. Gresham. *Christianity and Liberalism.* Reprint. Grand Rapids: William B. Eerdmans Publishing Co., 1983.

Murray, William J. *My Life Without God.* Nashville: Thomas Nelson Publishers, 1982.

Núñez C., Emilio A. *Liberation Theology.* Translated by Paul E. Sywulka. Chicago: Moody Press, 1985.

Schlossberg, Herbert. *Idols for Destruction: Christian Faith and Its Confrontation with American Society.* Nashville: Thomas Nelson Publishers, 1983.

Sproul, R. C. *The Psychology of Atheism.* Minneapolis: Bethany Fellowship, Inc., 1974.

Varghese, Roy Abraham, ed. *The Intellectuals Speak Out About God: A Handbook for the Christian in a Secular Society.* Foreword by Ronald Reagan. Chicago: Regnery Gateway, Inc., 1984.

IV. Coming to Terms with Temptation

Alcorn, Randy C. *Christians in the Wake of the Sexual Revolution: Recovering Our Sexual Sanity.* A Critical Concern Book. Portland: Multnomah Press 1985.

Bridges, Jerry. *The Pursuit of Holiness.* Colorado Springs: NavPress, 1978.

Busséll, Harold L. *Lord, I Can Resist Anything But Temptation.* Grand Rapids Pyranee Books, Zondervan Publishing House, 1985.

Carroll, Frances L. *Temptation: How Christians Can Deal with It.* Englewood Cliffs: Prentice-Hall, Inc., 1984.

Cerling, Charles, Jr. *Freedom from Bad Habits.* Foreword by Dwight Harvey Small. San Bernardino: Here's Life Publishers, Inc., 1984.

Kehl, D. G. *Control Yourself! Practicing the Art of Self-Discipline.* Grand Rapids: Zondervan Publishing House, 1982.

Lutzer, Erwin W. *How in This World Can I Be Holy?* Chicago: Moody Press 1985.

Lutzer, Erwin W. *How to Say No to a Stubborn Habit—Even When You Feel Like Saying Yes.* Foreword by Stuart Briscoe. Wheaton: Victor Books 1979.

Lutzer, Erwin W. *Living with Your Passions.* Foreword by Josh McDowell Wheaton: Victor Books, 1983.

Owen, John. *Sin and Temptation.* Edited and abridged by James M. Houston Introduction by J. I. Packer. Portland: Multnomah Press, 1983.

Petersen, J. Allan. *The Myth of the Greener Grass.* Wheaton: Tyndale House Publishers, Inc., 1983.

Swindoll, Charles R. *Moral Purity.* Fullerton: Insight for Living, 1985.

Swindoll, Charles R. *Sensuality: Resisting the Lure of Lust.* Portland Multnomah Press, 1981.

Walters, Richard P. *Jealousy, Envy, Lust: The Weeds of Greed.* Grand Rapids Pyranee Books, Zondervan Publishing House, 1985.

Wilson, Earl D. *Sexual Sanity: Breaking Free from Uncontrolled Habits.* Downers Grove: InterVarsity Press, 1984.

V. Coming to Terms with Leadership

Anderson, Robert C. *The Effective Pastor.* Chicago: Moody Press, 1985.

Baker, Don. *Leadership: Learning to Make Others Succeed.* Portland Multnomah Press, 1983.

Barber, Cyril J. *Nehemiah and the Dynamics of Effective Leadership.* Neptune: Loizeaux Brothers, 1976.

Barber, Cyril J., and Strauss, Gary H. *Leadership: The Dynamics of Success* Foreword by Dr. Vernon C. Grounds. Greenwood: The Attic Press, 1982.

Bratchard, Edward B. *The Walk-on-Water Syndrome.* Foreword by Wayne Oates. Waco: Word Books, 1984.

Campbell, Donald K. *Nehemiah: Man in Charge.* Wheaton: Victor Books 1979.

Eims, LeRoy. *Be a Motivational Leader.* Foreword by Charles R. Swindoll Wheaton: Victor Books, 1981.

Eims, LeRoy. *Be the Leader You Were Meant to Be.* Foreword by Theodore H. Epp. Wheaton: Victor Books, 1975.

Hocking, David L. *Be a Leader People Follow.* Ventura: Regal Books, 1979.

Peterson, Eugene H. *Five Smooth Stones for Pastoral Work.* Atlanta: John Knox Press, 1980.

Sanders, J. Oswald. *Paul the Leader.* Colorado Springs: NavPress, 1984.

Stott, John R. W. *The Preacher's Portrait: Some New Testament Word Studies.* Grand Rapids: William B. Eerdmans Publishing Co., 1961.

Sugden, Howard F., and Wiersbe, Warren W. *Confident Pastoral Leadership.* Chicago: Moody Press, 1973.

Swindoll, Charles R. *Hand Me Another Brick.* Nashville: Thomas Nelson Publishers, 1978.

Swindoll, Chuck. *Leadership.* Lifemaps series. Waco: Word Books, 1985.

VI. Coming to Terms with Aging

Conway, Jim. *Men in Mid-Life Crisis.* Elgin: David C. Cook Publishing Co., 1978.

Conway, Jim and Sally. *Women in Mid-Life Crisis.* Wheaton: Tyndale House Publishers, Inc., 1971.

Conway, Sally. *You and Your Husband's Mid-Life Crisis.* Elgin: David C. Cook Publishing Co., 1980.

Fabor, Heÿe. *Striking Sails: A Pastoral-Psychological View of Growing Older in Our Society.* Translated by Kenneth R. Mitchell. Nashville: Abingdon Press, 1984.

Fanning, Marilyn. *The Not So Golden Years: When Aging Parents Need Care.* Wheaton: Victor Books, 1984.

Hale, Charlotte. *The Super Years.* Old Tappan: Fleming H. Revell Co., 1984.

MacDonald, Gordon. *Living at High Noon: Reflections on the Dramas of Mid-Life.* Old Tappan: Fleming H. Revell Co., 1985.

Sell, Charles M. *Transition: The Stages of Adult Life.* Chicago: Moody Press, 1985.

White, Jerry and Mary. *The Christian in Mid-Life.* Colorado Springs: NavPress, 1980.

Wright, H. Norman. *The Seasons of a Marriage.* Ventura: Regal Books, 1982.

VII. Coming to Terms with Death

Anderson, J. Kerby. *Life, Death, and Beyond.* Grand Rapids: Zondervan Publishing House, 1980.

Attlee, Rosemary. *William's Story: A Mother's Account of Her Son's Struggle against Cancer.* Wheaton: Harold Shaw Publishers, 1983.

Bayly, Joseph. *The Last Thing We Talk About.* Rev. ed. Elgin: David C. Cook Publishing Co., 1973.

Dobihal, Edward F., Jr., and Stewart, Charles William. *When a Friend Is Dying: A Guide to Caring for the Terminally Ill and Bereaved.* Nashville: Abingdon Press, 1984.

Ford, Leighton. *Sandy: A Heart for God.* Downers Grove: InterVarsity Press, 1985.

Kreeft, Peter J. *Love Is Stronger Than Death.* San Francisco: Harper and Row, 1979.

Lewis, C. S. *A Grief Observed.* New York: The Seabury Press, 1961.

Manning, Doug. *Comforting Those Who Grieve: A Guide for Helping Others.* San Francisco: Harper and Row, 1985.

Manning, Doug. *Don't Take My Grief Away: What to Do When You Lose a Loved One.* Reprint. San Francisco: Harper and Row, 1984.

Means, James E. *A Tearful Celebration.* Portland: Multnomah Press, 1985.

Morey, Robert A. *Death and the Afterlife.* Foreword by Walter Martin. Minneapolis: Bethany House Publishers, 1984.

Nystrom, Carolyn. *What Happens When We Die?* Illustrated by Wayne A. Hanna. Children's Bible Basics. Chicago: Moody Press, 1981.

Richards, Larry, and Johnson, Paul, M. D. *Death and the Caring Community: Ministering to the Terminally Ill.* A Critical Concern Book. Portland: Multnomah Press, 1980.

Richardson, Jean. *A Death in the Family.* Belleville: Lion Publishing Corporation, 1985.

Sanford, Doris. *It Must Hurt A Lot: A Child's Book about Death.* Pictures by Graci Evans. Portland: Multnomah Press, 1985.

Sell, Charles M. *Grief's Healing Process: Understanding and Accepting Your Loss.* Portland: Multnomah Press, 1984.

Sherrill, John. *Mother's Song.* Grand Rapids: Chosen Books, The Zondervan Corporation, 1982.

Vanauken, Sheldon. *A Severe Mercy.* New York: Bantam Books, 1979.

Vredevelt, Pam W. *Empty Arms: Emotional Support for Those Who Have Suffered Miscarriage and Stillbirth.* Portland: Multnomah Press, 1984

VIII. Coming to Terms with Heaven and Hell

Bayly, Joseph. *Heaven.* Elgin: David C. Cook Publishing Co., 1977.

Chafer, Lewis Sperry. *Systematic Theology.* 8 vols. Dallas: Dallas Seminary Press, 1948.

Gerstner, John. *Jonathan Edwards on Heaven and Hell.* Grand Rapids: Baker Book House, 1980.

Harris, Murray J. *Raised Immortal: Resurrection and Immortality in the New Testament.* Grand Rapids: William B. Eerdmans Publishing Co., 1983

Hoyt, Herman A. *The End Times.* Chicago: Moody Press, 1969.

Kreeft, Peter J. *Heaven: The Heart's Deepest Longing.* San Francisco: Harper and Row, 1980.

Lewis, C. S. *The Great Divorce.* New York: Macmillan Publishing Co., Inc. 1946.

Lewis, C. S. *The Problem of Pain.* New York: Macmillan Publishing Co., Inc. 1962.

Shedd, William G. T. *Dogmatic Theology.* 3 vols. Reprint. Minneapolis: Klock and Klock Christian Publishers, 1979.

Thiessen, Henry C. *Lectures in Systematic Theology.* Revised by Vernon D Doerksen. Grand Rapids: William B. Eerdmans Publishing Co., 1979

Insight for Living
Cassette Tapes
LIVING ON THE RAGGED EDGE

How empty life can be ... how disillusioning ... how downright depressing! Yet, in all his under-the-sun counsel, Solomon finally comes back to the most foundational of all realities, the living God. You will feel as though someone has been looking through your journal as the pages of Ecclesiastes are unfolded. But best of all, you will realize that living on the ragged edge of life brings no satisfaction, no lasting pleasure. To find that, we must move above the sun into a vital relationship with the Son.

			U.S.	Canadian
LRE	CS	Cassette series—includes album cover	$65.25	$83.00
		Individual cassettes—include messages		
		A and B	5.00	6.35

These prices are effective as of December 1985 and are subject to change.

LRE   1-A: *Journal of a Desperate Journey*—Survey of Ecclesiastes
        B: *Chasing the Wind*—Ecclesiastes 1:1–18

LRE   2-A: *Eat, Drink, ... and Be* **What?**—Ecclesiastes 2:1–11
        B: *More Miles of Bad Road*—Ecclesiastes 2:12–26

LRE   3-A: *Do You Know What Time It Is?*—Ecclesiastes 3:1–11
        B: *Interlude of Rare Insight*—Ecclesiastes 3:11–15

LRE   4-A: *Confessions of a Cynic*—Ecclesiastes 3:16–22
        B: *The Lonely Whine of the Top Dog*—Ecclesiastes 4:1–8,
          Luke 12:15–21

LRE   5-A: *One Plus One Equals Survival*—Ecclesiastes 4:9–12
        B: *What Every Worshiper Should Remember*—Ecclesiastes 5:1–7

LRE   6-A: *Straight Talk to the Money-Mad*—Ecclesiastes 5:8–20
        B: *The Few Years of a Futile Life*—Ecclesiastes 6

LRE   7-A: *Wise Words for Busy People*—Ecclesiastes 7:1–14
        B: *Putting Wisdom to Work*—Ecclesiastes 7:15–29

LRE   8-A: *The Qualities of a Good Boss*—Ecclesiastes 8:1–9
        B: *Mysteries That Defy Explanation*—Ecclesiastes 8:10–17

LRE   9-A: *Have a Blast While You Last!*—Ecclesiastes 9:1–10
        B: *An Objective View of the Rat Race*—Ecclesiastes 9:11–18

LRE 10-A: *Be Sensible!*—Ecclesiastes 10:1–11
        B: *A Fool's Portrait*—Ecclesiastes 10:12–20

LRE 11-A: *Be Bullish!*—Ecclesiastes 11:1–6
        B: *Enjoying Life Now, Not Later*—Ecclesiastes 11:7–12:1

LRE 12-A: *Gray Hairs, Fewer Teeth, Yet a Big Smile*—Ecclesiastes 12:1–8
        B: *Wrapping Up a Ragged-Edge Journey*—Ecclesiastes 12:8–14

Ordering Information

U.S. ordering information: You are welcome to use our toll-free number (for orders only) between the hours of 8:30 A.M. and 4:00 P.M., Pacific Time, Monday through Friday. We can accept only Visa or MasterCard when ordering by phone. The number is (800) 772-8888. This number may be used anywhere in the continental United States excluding California, Hawaii, and Alaska. Orders from those areas are handled through our Sales Department at (714) 870-9161. We are unable to accept collect calls.

Your order will be processed promptly. We ask that you allow four to six weeks for delivery by fourth-class mail. If you wish your order to be shipped first-class, please add 10 percent of the total order (not including California sales tax) for shipping and handling.

Canadian ordering information: Your order will be processed promptly. We ask that you allow approximately four weeks for delivery by first-class mail to the U.S./Canadian border. All orders will be shipped from our office in Fullerton, California. For our listeners in British Columbia, a 7 percent sales tax must be added to the total of all tape orders (not including first-class postage). For further information, please contact our office at (604) 669-1916.

Payment options: We accept personal checks, money orders, Visa, and MasterCard in payment for materials ordered. Unfortunately, we are unable to offer invoicing or COD orders. If the amount of your check or money order is less than the amount of your purchase, your check will be returned so that you may place your order again with the correct amount. All orders must be paid in full before shipment can be made.

Returned checks: There is a $10 charge for any returned check (regardless of the amount of your order) to cover processing and invoicing.

Guarantee: Our tapes are guaranteed for ninety days against faulty performance or breakage due to a defect in the tape. For best results, please be sure your tape recorder is in good operating condition and is cleaned regularly.

Mail your order to one of the following addresses:

Insight for Living
Sales Department
Post Office Box 4444
Fullerton, CA 92634

Insight for Living Ministries
Post Office Box 2510
Vancouver, BC
Canada V6B 3W7

Quantity discounts and gift certificates are available upon request.

Overseas ordering information is provided on the reverse side of the order form.